D0132452

Specialties
of the House

A CULINARY COLLECTION

FROM THE FRIENDS AND REGENTS

OF THE KENMORE MUSEUM

The compilers of this book have taken every precaution to ensure that all recipes have been tried and tested but disclaim any responsibility for any error in quantities or ingredients. Attribution is given to chefs, restaurants and authors when recipe source information was available.

Photos are by Walter Smalling, Paul Beswick or Herb Barnett.

Additional copies of *Specialties of the House* may be obtained by contacting:

Specialties of the House
Kenmore Association, Inc.
1201 Washington Avenue
Fredericksburg, VA 22401
(703) 373-3381

Copyright © 1992 Kenmore Association, Inc., Fredericksburg, Virginia
Library of Congress Catalog Card Number 91-76796
ISBN 0-9631216-1-8

Printed in the USA by
WIMMER BROTHERS
A Wimmer Company
Memphis • Dallas

Table of Contents

A Note from the Editor

The Friends and Regents of the Kenmore Museum are happy to present you with this unique collection of recipes. Culled from our Regents, who represent most of the fifty states and England, these recipes illustrate a regional diversity that is characteristic of the Kenmore Association Inc.'s membership. My personal creations and selections from my favorite dining experiences round out our members' contributions. You will find here many well known chefs' and restaurants' choice dishes which have been adapted for your family's kitchen. And this wouldn't be a Kenmore cookbook without the recipe for our famous "Kenmore Gingerbread" and "Kenmore Fig Conserve" which we make available here so that you can recreate a bit of Kenmore in your own home.

A special thanks to Lois Stanton whose dedicated assistance in trying and testing many of the recipes helps assure that your efforts will turn out beautifully. Enjoy!

Carolyn Yorston

Chair: Cookbook Committee

Fielding Lewis (1725 - 1781)
by John Wollaston
"a gentleman of fortune and character…and much esteemed by the people, who would readily exert themselves under such a gentleman in case of a sudden call in the defense of our 'Frontier'."

Betty Washington Lewis (1733 - 1797)
by John Wollaston
"She was a most majestic looking woman, and so strikingly like her brother, that it was a matter of frolic to throw a cloak around her, and placing a military hat on her head, such was her amazing resemblance that on her appearance battalions would have presented arms and senates risen to do honor to the chief." Quote from George Washington Parke Custis.

Preface

Few American houses have so rich and varied a culinary tradition as Kenmore. Through wars and hard times alike visitors have enjoyed its hospitality in full measure, good food and drink, gaiety and laughter. Today it is still easy to imagine the Marquis de Lafayette enjoying gingerbread (and whiskey!) with Mary Washington, and the balls and barbecues described by Washington during his frequent visits to his "Sister Lewis."

Kenmore is one of the nation's oldest museum houses. Since 1922 its doors have been open to visitors from all over the world who come to see its superb collection and the breathtaking artistry of the mansion's decorative plasterwork, or to enjoy wide-ranging artistic and cultural events.

The handsome Georgian mansion was built on rising land to the west of Fredericksburg, Virginia, just before the American Revolution. Its builder, Col. Fielding Lewis, had married first Catharine, cousin of George Washington, and then Betty, his sister.

Capt. John Smith described the scene at the Falls of the Rappahannock River in 1608: "Heaven and earth never agreed better to frame a place for man's habitation." When the Lewises moved into their new house, rich farm lands still lay all around.

Fredericksburg was the childhood home of George Washington. It was across the Rappahannock (not the Potomac) that the legendary silver dollar was thrown, and that doomed cherry tree of another Parson Weems story could only have stood at Ferry Farm, across the river from the wharves and storehouses of the bustling colonial port. To this day, cherry pie contests are held to mark the birthday of the Father of His Country and Fredericksburg's favorite son.

Washington and his sister, Betty Lewis, remained close throughout their lives. In 1775 they even shared the skills of a "stoco man" who created lavish decorative plasterwork at Kenmore and at Mount Vernon. This plasterwork, repaired and embellished with great skill by Key Howard in 1883, remains the glory of the house. It is brimming with appetizing images: clusters of grapes (for summer) in the "Four Seasons" ceiling, cornucopias spilling flowers and fruit over the long banquet table in the dining room, and, in the elaborate Aesop's Fable chimney piece, a delectable piece of cheese hanging forever suspended in its fall from the mouth of the crow, tricked into song by the flattering fox.

Colonel Lewis was an early and ardent supporter of American independence. He operated and financed a gunnery to arm the American troops. This unsung patriot died only a week after the victory at Yorktown, leaving his widow in dire financial straits. But even during the hardships of the Revolution and the lean years that followed, Betty Washington Lewis' gaiety and courage are evident. She was fond of sending her brother "honey in the comb," which he loved. And there is a charming account of Mrs. Lewis and other women of Fredericksburg entertaining, in 1778, a group of imprisoned Hessian officers at an afternoon musicale where they served "tea, wine and cakes!"

But by 1796 Mrs. Lewis was writing to her brother, "I am obliged to buy everything that I eat with the addition of soap, candles, etc. in short the most trifling things." For a Virginia plantation owner this was a sad state of affairs.

After Betty Lewis' death in 1797 the house passed to the Barton family and then, in 1819, to the Gordons, who named the house "Kenmore" after their ancestral seat in Scotland. In 1833 the Gordons played host to President Andrew Jackson and to Washington Irving after the dedication of the first Mary Washington Monument. A second monument was dedicated in 1895.

After the tragic years of the War Between the States, when Kenmore was badly damaged during the

Battle of Fredericksburg, the fate of the house seemed uncertain. But the Howard family purchased it in 1881, and, soon afterward their remarkably talented son, Key, began his restoration and embellishment of the plasterwork.

Located near an outcropping of rock, not far from Kenmore, stood the Mary Washington Monument, the final resting place of George Washington's and Betty Washington Lewis' mother. By the 1890's the monument had become derelict. Thanks to the efforts of the ladies of Fredericksburg, a second monument was created to honor the memory of Washington's mother. These efforts by the Fredericksburg women paved the way for women's leadership in preservation movements throughout America. The second monument was dedicated with great pomp and ceremony—and prodigious amounts of food! Mrs. V. M. Fleming, who would later lead in restoring Kenmore, describes the lunch given there for President Grover Cleveland: "Bread of all kinds, ham, broiled chicken, tomatoes stuffed with chicken salad and placed on lettuce leaves and covered with mayonnaise dressing, pickles and coffee for the first course. For the second course, strawberries and ice cream and old fashioned pound cake with thick heavy icing." For the "Ladies of the Association" who had planned all this, a "hurried, simple" lunch had to suffice: "tomatoes and lettuce and mayonnaise, an elegant saddle of mutton, bread and butter and beaten biscuits and wafers, coffee and iced tea and chocolate cake...besides currant jelly, pickles, delightful ham and tongue and also fruitcake which we entirely forgot to put on the table in the hurry." Light lunches were definitely not the style of old Fredericksburg and Kenmore!

By 1922, Kenmore had again fallen on hard times. The property was offered for development, which would almost certainly have ensured the destruction of the house. In May of that year, Mrs. Fleming (of the hurried lunch), her energetic daughter, "Miss Annie" Smith, and other women of Fredericksburg organized the Kenmore Association.

Their success, based on organization and teamwork, was phenomenal, even during the Depression. Much of that success centered on the pleasures of the table. Minutes of the early meetings are filled with appointments to the Fried Chicken Committee, the Tossed Salad Committee, or to its necessary subcommittee, French Dressing. These ardent fundraisers (in cooperation with the Committees for Ham, Potato Salad and Pound Cake) carried Kenmore from the brink of destruction to an assured continuance of dignity and beauty in an endless round of teas, luncheons and dinners on the grounds. To this day, many a Fredericksburg woman remembers getting a midnight call from Miss Annie instructing her to "bring two fried chickens to the lunch tomorrow at Kenmore" and then, upon her sleepy acquiescence, the parting shot..."On second thought, bring four!"

The founding of the national Board of Regents in 1925, under the leadership of Louise duPont Crowninshield, ensured Kenmore's growth and development as one of the nation's greatest historic houses. Hospitality and tradition have remained the keynote. When a "colonial kitchen" was constructed on the foundation of the original structure, the ladies of Kenmore decided that all visitors must be served refreshments. And what could be more appropriate than the legendary recipe for gingerbread passed down from Mary Washington herself to many of the ladies of Fredericksburg? It was this gingerbread which "Mother Washington" had been baking when Lafayette paid her a surprise visit. The "Lafayette Gingerbread," with a cup of tea, is one of all visitors' memories of Kenmore.

Kenmore continues to grow and develop. The museum sponsors innovative educational programs for children, musical and theatrical programs, lectures and workshops. It also continues to convey a sense of life's true pleasures—not the least being the pleasures of the table!

Education Programs at Kenmore

"How many batteries go in that big clock?" asks a third grader as he listens to the ticking of the tall case clock in the passage at Kenmore. Young visitors learn about eighteenth-century technology and culture by exploring the sights, sounds, smells and textures at Kenmore.

Guides lead discussions in the Mansion and activities in the Hands On Room. As kindergarteners go through the Mansion, they look for objects named in familiar nursery rhymes, reciting the verses after discovering Polly's kettle, Jack's candlestick, or Humpty Dumpty's egg cup. They hold reproduction pieces of plaster ornaments as they search for identical castings on the ceilings. Older students count fireplaces in the Mansion and in the Hands-On Room; they learn to lay a fire, design their own plaster overmantel, and build with brick. Students visit the milliner's shop in the role of eighteenth-century shoppers, select hats or wigs such as Fielding Lewis would have worn, and then buy or barter for them. After seeing eighteenth-century teaware in the Mansion, students may set their own tea table in the Hands-On Room and then enjoy a cup of tea and slice of gingerbread when visiting the colonial kitchen.

Hands-On tours for visually impaired visitors allow them to discover Kenmore with their fingertips. Examining a floor plan of the Mansion outlined in velcro, they can understand the arrangement of rooms, doors and windows. When passed among the visitors, a scale section of the drawing room ceiling, with its garlands of plaster flowers and leaves, brings the ornamental plasterwork within their reach.

Kenmore's "hands-on" approach to learning has opened new doors to the past for school children and the visually impaired. Their visit to Kenmore allows them to touch history and history to touch them, in a new way.

In the Hands-On Room, students study pictures of eighteenth-century life and then recreate the scenes using reproduction objects.

Acknowledgements

KENMORE ASSOCIATION, INC. BOARD OF REGENTS

Mrs. Richard S. Aldrich	Rhode Island	Mrs. Russell Fortune	Indiana
Mrs. P. Kelley Armour	Illinois	Mrs. Robert L. Frackelton	Virginia
Mrs. M. Edward Bacon	Nevada	Mrs. Richard W. Freeman	Louisiana
Mrs. Frederick G. Bannerot, Jr.	West Virginia	Mrs. Launce Gamble	California
Mrs. Joseph C. Bennett	Utah	Mrs. J. Frank Gerrity	Maine
Mrs. James Billups	Texas	Mrs. B. Douglas Goff	Kentucky
Mrs. Alfred E. Bissell	Delaware	Mrs. Hunter Goodrich	New York
Mrs. Henry V. Blaxter, Jr.	Pennsylvania	Mrs. Downey M. Gray	Kentucky
Mrs. Mary Katherine Blount	Alabama	Mrs. G. Gardiner Green	Mississippi
Mrs. John D. Bryson	Wisconsin	Mrs. P. Benjamin Grosscup	Pennsylvania
Mrs. N. S. Calhoun	Florida	Mrs. Arthur Hall	Nevada
Mrs. Simon B. D. Cardew	California	Mrs. Frederic C. Hamilton	Colorado
Mrs. Lucius Clay, Jr.	Virginia	Mrs. Gordon Hanes	North Carolina
Mrs. Edward B. Close, Jr.	Colorado	Mrs. Quintin T. Hardtner	Louisiana
Mrs. Harry B. Combs	Arizona	Mrs. David F. Harris	Connecticut
Mrs. Nancy D. Cudahy	Wisconsin	Mrs. Patrick Healy	Maryland
Mrs. Bratton Davis	South Carolina	Mrs. James M.Hewgley	Oklahoma
Mrs. George H. Dunklin	Arkansas	Mrs. E. Chipman Higgins	Hawaii
Mrs. George S. Ebbert, Jr.	Pennsylvania	Mrs. Charles F. Hovey	Massachusetts
Mrs. John Handy Edwards	Oklahoma	Mrs. John A. Howell	Texas
Mrs. D. Trowbridge Elliman	Vermont	Mrs. Meriwether Hudson	North Carolina
Mrs. Harold M. Esty	New York	Mrs. Hugo G. Huettig	District of Columbia
Mrs. Daniel B. Evans	Pennsylvania	Mrs. Joseph C. Hutcheson	Texas
Mrs. James P. Evans	Mississippi	Mrs. D. Eldredge Jackson	Rhode Island
Mrs. William H. Evans	Ohio	Mrs. T. Story Jenks	Vermont
Mrs. John L. Fenlon	Virginia	Mrs. James F. Jennings	New Mexico
Mrs. James Ficklen, Jr.	North Carolina	Mrs. E. Leon Keith	Wyoming
Mrs. William H. Flowers	Georgia	Mrs. David F. King	Virginia

Mrs. Denison Kitchel	Arizona	Mrs. Austin B. Sayre	New Jersey
Mrs. Walter J. Laird	Delaware	Mrs. William C. Schock	Missouri
Mrs. H. Gordon Leggett	Virginia	Mrs. Eustace K. Shaw	Iowa
Mrs. Edward B. Linthicum	Texas	Mrs. Edward D. Sloan	South Carolina
Mrs. Ernest T. Livingstone	Oregon	Mrs. W. Holt Souder	Virginia
Mrs. David H. Marbury	Alabama	Mrs. John W. Starr	Texas
Mrs. Malcolm Matheson, Jr.	District of Columbia	Mrs. R. Ted Steinbock	Kentucky
Mrs. Ruth Mathews	Arizona	Mrs. George Steiner	Minnesota
Mrs. James B. Maytag	Colorado	Mrs. Harry F. Stimpson	Minnesota
Mrs. John T. Nightingale	Massachusetts	Mrs. Franz T. Stone	At Large
Mrs. Lawrence A. Norton	Massachusetts	Mary, Countess of Strathmore	Great Britain
Mrs. Eric Oldberg	Illinois	Mrs. George H. Taber	Maine
Mrs. Robert D. Orr	Indiana	Mrs. Lilburn T. Talley	Virginia
Mrs. Jacque Ostheimer	New Mexico	Mrs. Frederick C. Tanner	Connecticut
Mrs. Thomas R. Pansing	Nebraska	Mrs. L. Newton Thomas	West Virginia
Mrs. William M. Passano	Maryland	Mrs. Edward A. Thompson	Tennessee
Mrs. Burleigh Pattee	At Large	Mrs. Robert E. Tipton	Arkansas
Mrs. Andrew Price, Jr.	Washington	Mrs. Robert VanDervoort	Nebraska
Mrs. Wiley R. Reynolds	Florida	Mrs. Paul J. Vignos	Ohio
Mrs. William C. Ridgway, Jr.	New Jersey	Mrs. Brooks Walker	California
Mrs. Luis Emilio Rinaldini	New York	Mrs. Jeffrey L. Walters	Michigan
Mrs. James D. Robinson	Georgia	Mrs. Robert C. Warren	Oregon
Mrs. Kip Robinson	Missouri	Mrs. Alexander W. Wellford	Tennessee
Mrs. Conrad Ruckelshaus	Indiana	Mrs. Clinton R. Wyckoff	New York
Mrs. Calvin Satterfield, III	Virginia	Mrs. Carolyn Yorston	California

Space precludes the inclusion of all the delicious recipes that were submitted, but the compilers of this cookbook acknowledge the Regents of Kenmore and the following friends of the Kenmore Museum for their interest and their help:

Mr. Walter O. Angel

Mrs. Ned Barclay Ball (Grace)

Mrs. Robert Biddle, III (Sally)

Mrs. Donn Campbell

Mrs. Denton A. Cooley

Mrs. Shirley Corriher

Mrs. William A. Crabill (Marjorie)

Mr. Vernon Edenfield

Ms. Frances M. Folsom

Mrs. Clay Haymes (Katherine)

Mrs. Clement F. Haynsworth, Jr. (Dorothy)

Mrs. Jon Jenkins (Fran)

Mrs. Lynn Johnson (Sandy)

Anne Lewis

Ms. Laurel McLean

Mrs. Alan More-Nisbet

Mrs. Daniel F. Norton

Mrs. Farquhar Ogilvie

Ms. Jacque Otero

Mrs. Howard B. Peabody (Peggy)

Ms. Lyn Phillips

Mrs. Paul E. Sackett (Bessie)

Mrs. Alger Shelden (Frances)

Ms. Demaris Skouras

Mrs. James A. Simpson (Florence)

Ms. Charlotte Smith

Mrs. John E. Smith (Mabel)

Ms. John Smith

Mrs. William Stanton (Lois)

Mrs. Jerrie Strom

Mrs. Michael Terkel (Liselotte)

Mr. Burt Tysinger

Mrs. Benjamin N. Wafle (Kitty Lee)

Mrs. Fielding L. Williams (Susan)

Recipes from the following chefs, restaurateurs, and authors were recommended for inclusion in this cookbook. Every effort has been made to credit when possible:

Lee Bailey

Simone Beck

Giuliano Bugialli

Cal-A-Vie, The Ultimate Spa, Vista, California

Jamie Davies, *Chef Schramsberg Cellars*, St. Helena, California

Marcel Desaulniers, *The Trellis Cafe, Restaurant and Grill*, Williamsburg, Virginia

John Downey, *Chef Downey's*, Santa Barbara, California

The Galisteo Inn, Galisteo, New Mexico

Freddy Girardet, *Chef Girardet's*, Crissier, Switzerland

The Golden Door, Fitness Resort, Escondido, California

Joyce Goldstein, *Chef/Owner, Square One*, San Francisco, California

Marcella Hazan

Justine's Restaurant, Midland, Michigan

Madeleine Kamman

John Makin, *Chef, Duckworth Restaurant*, St. Helena, California

Chef Bill Neal, *Crook's Corner*, Chapel Hill, North Carolina

Mme. Jeanette Pepin

Larry Vito, *Chef, Stanford Court*, San Francisco, California

Alice Waters, *Chef/Owner, Chez Panisse*, Berkeley, California

Anne Willan, *La Barenne Cooking School*, Paris, France

Kenmore

Come dine with me,
I'll share the memories
of my years
when candles glowed
in every room
and I was young,
my praises sung
by Washington himself.

I watched the Blue and Gray,
my windows high
above the fields,
and saw the ones
I loved die young,
still served the wine
and laid the table
for the next to come.

My walls are strong,
my plaster ceilings
wear their beauty well,
the silver shines,
fine glass reflects
the fire's glow,
come dine with me,
there is so much
for you to know.

Antonia B. Laird

*"There is no love sincerer
than the love of food."*

George Bernard Shaw

$\mathcal{A}$ppetizers

These wine glasses, the punch pot for brewing and serving hot punch
and the tray are from the Kenmore collection. Documents show that the
Lewises owned a mahogany tea board, and archaeologists have
uncovered fragments of black transfer-printed creamware and air twist
wine glass stems.

Deviled Egg Ball

Serves 8 to 10

10 hard cooked eggs

3 green onions, tops included, cut into 2-inch pieces

⅓ cup mayonnaise

½ teaspoon salt

¼ teaspoon pepper

½ teaspoon dill weed

2 teaspoons Dijon-style mustard

Topping:

3 ounces cream cheese at room temperature

2 tablespoons mayonnaise

Garnishes:

Lettuce leaves

1 2-ounce can sliced black olives

Pumpernickel bread rounds or crackers

- In bowl of food processor with steel blade, place green onions and mince. With processor running, drop eggs through the feed tube one at a time until mashed. Turn off food processor. Add mayonnaise and seasonings, use pulse motion just to blend.

- Place egg mixture into a 2½ cup round mixing bowl that has been lined with plastic wrap. Refrigerate overnight.

• • •

- To serve, run knife around the edges and unmold onto lettuce-lined serving tray. Combine cream cheese and 2 tablespoons mayonnaise until smooth. Use this to frost the egg ball. Cover the frosted egg ball with sliced black olives. Serve with bread rounds or crackers.

Variation: Of course, caviar can be used to garnish instead of black olives. For Easter use one-half of a large plastic egg for an oval mold.

"Being kissed by a man who didn't wax his moustache was like eating an egg without salt."

Rudyard Kipling

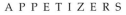
Almond-Mushroom Pâté

Makes 2 cups

2 tablespoons butter

½ small onion, chopped

1 clove garlic, minced

½ pound mushrooms, coarsely chopped

Dash salt

Dash white pepper

½ teaspoon chopped fresh tarragon (or ¼ teaspoon dried tarragon, crushed)

1 8-ounce jar almond butter

1 tablespoon dry sherry

1 tablespoon whipping cream

Whole blanched almonds for garnish

- Melt butter in medium skillet. Add onion, garlic, mushrooms, salt, pepper and tarragon. Cook, stirring occasionally, until most of the liquid has evaporated.

- In food processor or blender, combine almond butter, mushroom mixture, sherry and cream. Process until smooth. Turn out onto serving dish. Cover and chill.

- Garnish with whole, blanched almonds and serve on whole wheat toast or crackers.

Light and Easy Tuna Party Pâté

Makes 3½ cups

8 ounces low-calorie cream cheese

3 tablespoons chili sauce

3 tablespoons minced fresh parsley

1 tablespoon minced scallions (or onion)

2 6½-ounce cans water-packed tuna, drained

- Combine ingredients in a food processor, using the steel blade. Process until smooth. Pack into a 4-cup mold or a round bottom bowl lined with plastic wrap. Cover and chill until firm. Unmold on a bed of lettuce, or party tray. Serve with crackers.

Parmesan Toasts

Serves 12 to 16

1 loaf very thin bread

8 tablespoons butter (1 stick)

2 cloves garlic

½ pound freshly grated Parmesan cheese

- Preheat oven to 350°.

- Trim crusts from the bread and cut in rectangular halves. Spread bread in a single layer on a jelly roll pan. Do not leave spaces between the bread slices.

- Coarsely chop the garlic and add to the butter. Melt the butter. Remove the garlic after it has flavored the butter. Brush the butter over the bread slices, and sprinkle with the Parmesan cheese.

- Place pan in the preheated oven. Bake until really browned and crusted.

Almond Parmesan Fingers

3 tablespoons chopped almonds

3 tablespoons butter

6 tablespoons grated Parmesan cheese

3 tablespoons heavy cream

3 tablespoons minced parsley

Salt

Pepper

12 buttered toast strips

- Preheat oven to 350°.

- Blanch and chop almonds. Sauté in butter until golden brown.

- Combine Parmesan cheese, heavy cream and parsley. Season with salt and pepper to taste. Spread this cheese mixture on toast strips. Place in 350° oven for 5 to 8 minutes to heat thoroughly.

Sesame Cheese Wafers

Makes 4 dozen

½ **pound grated Tillamook cheese**

2 **tablespoons soft butter**

¾ **cup flour**

1 **teaspoon Worcestershire sauce**

½ **teaspoon salt**

Dash of liquid hot pepper seasoning

¼ **cup sesame seeds**

- Combine grated cheese with butter, flour, Worcestershire sauce, salt and liquid red pepper seasoning. Mix thoroughly.

- Form the cheese dough into 1-inch diameter logs. Roll in sesame seeds, gently pressing the seeds into the dough. Wrap in foil and refrigerate until cold enough to slice about ⅛-inch thick. Place on cookie sheets.

- Preheat oven to 450°. Bake wafers for about 10 minutes. Watch closely so they do not burn.

Note: If you like, more sesame seeds can be pressed onto the surface of the wafers just before baking.

Note: The cheese dough freezes very well.

Variations: For a south-of-the-border wafer, use Monterey Jack cheese and add 1 tablespoon finely minced jalapeño peppers with seeds and veins removed.

For Italian-flavored wafers, use 4-ounces freshly grated Parmesan cheese and 4-ounces grated Provolone cheese and 1 tablespoon fresh basil or oregano finely minced (or 2 teaspoons dried herbs).

Josefinas

Makes about 30

8 hard French-style rolls

1 cup fresh Anaheim or California chilies, seeds and veins removed (or 1 cup canned green chilies)

1 cup butter

1 clove garlic, minced

1 cup mayonnaise

8 ounces Monterey Jack cheese, grated

- Slice rolls (or French bread) into ½-inch slices, and toast on one side.

- Chop chilies and mix with butter and garlic. Spread the chili mixture on the untoasted sides of bread slices.

- Mix mayonnaise and cheese and spread on the bread. Broil until cheese is brown and puffy. Serve at once.

Note: These may be served as an appetizer or with a Mexican menu or any casserole supper.

Note: The chili butter mixture by itself is good spread on grilled fish or chicken.

Cheese Puffs

Makes 24

¾ cup (about ¼ pound) grated cheese (Cheddar or cream cheese mixed with some Roquefort)

1 egg white

Small amount of heavy cream

French bread slices about ¼-inch thick

- Soften cheese to room temperature. Combine with a little cream to a spreadable consistency.

- Beat egg white until stiff but not dry. Fold egg white into the cheese mixture.

- Toast the bread rounds on one side. Dollop cheese mixture on untoasted side. Place in a 400° oven until cheese puffs and browns slightly. Serve at once.

Roquefort Canapés

Makes 3 dozen

6 ounces Roquefort or blue cheese

2 egg whites, beaten

Melba toast rounds

- Preheat broiler. Cream the cheese in a small mixing bowl with a wooden spoon. Beat the egg whites until stiff and blend with the cheese. Spread mixture on Melba toast rounds, heaping it slightly.

- Place on a cookie sheet and toast under the broiler for about five minutes, or until cheese is puffed and browned.

Croquettes De Brie Avec Poivre Noir
(Fried Wedges of Peppered Brie)

Serves 6

1 pound ripe Brie cheese

Freshly ground black peppercorns (coarse grind)

2 tablespoons all-purpose flour

1 egg, beaten

6 tablespoons fine, dry white breadcrumbs

Vegetable oil for deep fryer

- Cut the Brie into wedges and roll them in the ground peppercorns. Dust each piece with flour. Then coat each piece with egg and roll in breadcrumbs. Coat with egg and roll in breadcrumbs again.

- Heat the vegetable oil in a deep fryer to 375°. In a basket, deep-fry the croquettes for 2 minutes. Drain on paper towels and serve hot.

Note: Gerard Pangaud recommends this peppered Brie with a fine burgundy or Cabernet Sauvignon.

Phyllo Wrapped Brie

Serves 20

12 sheets phyllo pastry

1 pound sweet, unsalted butter, melted

1 wheel Brie cheese, about 5 pounds, not fully ripened

- Place Brie in the freezer for 30 minutes before preparation.

- Butter a baking sheet large enough to hold the Brie.

- Lay five sheets of phyllo on the baking sheet, brushing melted butter on each layer. Set Brie on top of the phyllo and fold edges up around the cheese.

- Cover top of the cheese with six sheets of phyllo, brushing melted butter on each layer. Tuck ends of pastry under the cheese. Brush top and sides with butter.

- Preheat oven to 350°. Fold last sheet of phyllo in a long one-inch strip, brush with butter, form into a flower shape on top of the Brie and again brush with butter. (Flower may be omitted and just brush with butter.)

- Bake 20 to 30 minutes or until golden brown. Let stand 30 minutes before serving.

Rolled Soufflé

¼ cup flour

1 cup milk

2 egg yolks

Salt and freshly ground white pepper

3 egg whites

Fillings:

Creamed chicken, ham, crabmeat or spinach.

Cream cheese, thinned with milk, and caviar.

Smoked salmon mousse: Purée 5-ounces smoked salmon and combine with ½ cup heavy cream, whipped. Season with freshly ground white pepper. Press through a fine sieve. Spread on the soufflé, a line of red caviar can be made down the center of the roll.

- Preheat oven to 375°.

- Line a jelly roll pan with aluminum foil. Butter and flour-dust the pan.

- Prepare a panade by stirring flour and ¼ cup of the milk in a saucepan to make a thick paste. Add remaining milk and cook over medium heat until the sauce thickens.

- Remove from heat and add the egg yolks, stirring vigorously. Add seasonings.

- Beat egg whites until stiff but not dry. Fold into the sauce.

- Spread soufflé mixture on the prepared pan. Bake in preheated oven for 20 to 25 minutes.

- Remove soufflé from the oven, cover with a damp towel. Invert. Peel off foil and roll soufflé, starting with the longer side, in the damp towel. Cool.

•   •   •

- When soufflé is cool, unroll and fill.

Note: Cheese can be added to the soufflé mixture for variety.

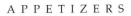

Soufflés Another Way

Serves 4 to 6

2½ tablespoons butter

⅓ cup flour

1¾ cups milk

½ teaspoon salt

¼ teaspoon freshly ground pepper

Pinch of nutmeg, freshly grated

1½ cups grated Swiss cheese

5 large eggs, lightly beaten with a fork

- Preheat oven to 375°. Butter and flour-dust a 1-quart soufflé dish. Refrigerate until ready to fill.

- In a small saucepan melt the butter; add the flour and cook, stirring with a whisk, for about 1 minute.

- Add the milk to the roux, bring to a boil, whisking as it thickens. Remove from heat.

- Add the cheese and mix well. Cool for a few moments before adding the beaten eggs.

- Fill the prepared mold with the mixture and set aside until ready to bake.

- Bake in the preheated oven for 40 to 45 minutes. Serve immediately.

Note: Serve as a first course for dinner or as a luncheon dish with a salad.

Variations: Add chopped fresh cooked vegetables, use any variety of sharp cheese, jalapeño cheese, seafood, chicken, puréed cooked spinach, carrots, cauliflower, broccoli, celery, fennel or celery root.

Serve with a celery sauce, cream tomato sauce, creamy pesto sauce, red pepper sauce or any compatible sauce of your choice.

Napoleon De Roquefort

Serves 6

1 pound puff pastry dough

½ pound Roquefort cheese

1 scant teaspoon powdered gelatin

2 tablespoons sauternes or other good dessert wine

1 cup heavy cream, whipped

1 ounce English walnuts, chopped

- Preheat oven to 400°. Roll the puff pastry into a very thin rectangle, about 10" x 12". Place the dough on a baking sheet and prick with a fork in a few places to permit steam to escape. Bake in preheated oven until well risen and golden brown on top, about 15 minutes. Cool.

- In a blender or food processor, beat the Roquefort cheese until it is creamy. Add the gelatin to the sauternes in a small pan and warm over low heat until the gelatin is dissolved.

- Fold the gelatin mixture into the Roquefort. Then fold in the whipped cream.

- With a sharp knife, cut the puff pastry into three strips of equal size, about 4" x 10". Spread half of the Roquefort cream on one strip. Cover with a second strip and spread it with the remaining Roquefort cream. Cover with the third piece of puff pastry. Sprinkle walnuts on top. Chill in the refrigerator to set the Roquefort cream and hold until serving time. Serve in slices about 1½-inches thick.

Note: Gerard Pangaud, chef de cuisine Aurora restaurant in New York suggests a fine sauternes or other rich dessert wine with this cheese course.

New Potatoes with Golden Caviar

Serves 12

24 very small new potatoes

2 tablespoons olive oil

½ cup sour cream

4 ounces golden caviar

- In a 400° oven, bake the potatoes in their jackets for about 25 minutes. Cut in half, scoop out pulp, and roughly mash the pulp with a fork. Brush the insides of the potatoes with the olive oil; turn upside down on baking sheet and bake in 475° oven for 10 to 15 minutes, or until crisp.

- Fill the potato shells with the potato pulp which has been mixed with the sour cream. Dollop with caviar and serve hot.

Spinach Tartare

Serves 6 to 8

2 10-ounce packages frozen chopped spinach

6 green onions, tops included, cut in 2-inch pieces

1 heaping handful parsley leaves

2 teaspoons salt

1 teaspoon coarsely ground pepper (be generous)

⅔ cup mayonnaise

- Thaw spinach but do not cook. In the bowl of a food processor with the steel blade, coarsely chop the green onions and the parsley. Add the spinach and pulse to chop coarsely. Season with salt and pepper, and add enough mayonnaise to bind the ingredients and make the tartare spreadable. Serve as a spread with crackers.

Note: If using fresh spinach, steam briefly to wilt but not to cook.

Variation: To use this mixture as a dip, add more mayonnaise and some sour cream.

Stuffed Mushrooms

Serves 8

1 shallot, minced

½ pound mushrooms, finely chopped

2 teaspoons butter

⅛ cup low-fat milk

16 mushroom caps

2 tablespoons grated Gruyère cheese (or another good Swiss cheese)

White wine

- In a medium skillet, sweat shallot in butter, but do not brown. Add chopped mushrooms and cook on low heat until moisture has evaporated. Add milk, heat to warm. Let cool.

- Stuff mushroom caps with ½ tablespoon mixture. Top each with ½ teaspoon grated cheese.

- Just before serving, heat oven to 450°. Place mushrooms in shallow pan. Sprinkle with white wine and bake for 5 minutes. Serve immediately.

Note: This is a delicious low calorie appetizer. Two mushrooms per serving equals 29 calories per serving.

Shrimp Stuffed Celery

Serves 10 to 12

½ pound cooked shrimp

½ cup sweet pickle relish

2 teaspoons horseradish

6 tablespoons mayonnaise

2 tablespoons grated onion

20 to 24 2-inch pieces celery ribs

- Chop the shrimp and combine with the relish, horseradish, mayonnaise and onion.

- Fill the celery boats with the shrimp mixture and serve.

Marinated Shrimp and Mushrooms

Serves 8 to 10

2 pounds cooked medium shrimp

1 pound medium mushrooms

½ cup oil

½ cup wine vinegar

½ cup sugar

1 tablespoon fresh dill

1 clove minced garlic

1 tablespoon chopped fresh basil

2 teaspoons salt

1 tablespoon freshly ground pepper

1 tablespoon freshly chopped parsley

1 large onion, thinly sliced

2 teaspoons lemon juice

- Combine all ingredients in a large jar. Marinate for 24 hours. Shake jar 2 or 3 times a day.

- One hour before serving remove shrimp, onion rings and mushrooms from the marinade. Place in lettuce-lined bowl.

Hawaiian Sesame Shrimp

Serves 8

1 tablespoon sesame seeds

2 tablespoons sesame oil

2 tablespoons vegetable oil

1 pound medium shrimp, shelled and deveined

½ cup chopped green onion

½ teaspoon salt (optional)

¼ teaspoon freshly ground black pepper

1 tablespoon brown sugar

1 tablespoon soy sauce

- Preheat oven to 300°. Toast sesame seeds on baking sheet until golden brown.

- Heat oils in heavy saucepan over high heat. Add shrimp, onion, salt, pepper and sugar. Stir-fry for 1 to 3 minutes. Reduce heat to low, add soy sauce and stir.

- Remove from heat and sprinkle with sesame seeds. Serve hot.

Louisiana Pickled Shrimp

Serves 10 to 12

3 pounds raw medium-sized shrimp

3 large white onions, thinly sliced

8 bay leaves

1 cup extra virgin olive oil

¾ cup white wine vinegar

5 teaspoons celery seed

3 teaspoons salt

- Shell and devein shrimp. Bring a large pot of water to a boil, plunge shrimp into the boiling water and cook just until the shrimp turn opaque and pink (do not over cook). Immediately rinse shrimp under cold running water.

- In a large glass bowl, layer the shrimp, sliced onion and bay leaves. Repeat layers until all shrimp are used, ending with onions.

- Combine the olive oil, vinegar, celery seed and salt. Pour over the shrimp. Cover tightly and allow to "pickle" for 5 to 6 hours.

Variation: You may use half shrimp and half scallops.

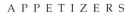

Chili Appetizer

Serves 6

1 small can jalapeño chilies en escabeche

1 3-ounce package cream cheese, room temperature

1 tablespoon sour cream

1 tablespoon minced onion

¼ cup shredded crabmeat (fresh shrimp, minced, or water-packed albacore tuna may be substituted)

- Preheat oven to 400°.

- Remove seeds from the chilies and rinse and drain. Mash sour cream and cream cheese together, adding a bit more sour cream if necessary. Blend in the onion and the crab, shrimp or tuna.

- Neatly spoon the filling into each chili. Place in the preheated oven for 10 minutes or until filling has been heated and is slightly puffed.

Variation: This same filling can be used to fill mushroom caps which have been wiped clean with a damp paper towel. Fill the mushroom caps and bake only 8 minutes or they will begin to exude liquid and collapse because of the overcooking.

Super Nachos

Serves 10 to 12

½ **pound lean ground beef**

½ **pound chorizo sausage, casing removed (available in Mexican markets, if unavailable use a total of 1 pound lean ground beef)**

1 large onion, chopped

Salt

Liquid hot pepper seasoning

1 or 2 cans (about 1 pound each) refried beans (or make your own with pinto beans)

1 4-ounce can whole California green chilies, remove seeds and veins

2 to 3 cups shredded Monterey Jack or mild Cheddar cheese (or a combination)

¾ **cup prepared taco sauce (green or red or both)**

Garnishes:

¼ **cup chopped green onions, including tops**

1 cup pitted ripe olives

1 8-ounce can thawed avocado dip or 1 avocado, peeled, pitted, and coarsely mashed

1 cup sour cream

1 mild red pickled pepper

Cilantro sprigs

8 cups tortilla chips or corn-flavored chips

- Crumble ground beef and chorizo in a skillet. Add onion and cook on high heat, stirring, until meat is lightly browned. Discard fat, season with salt and liquid hot pepper seasoning to taste.

- Spread refried beans in a shallow 10" x 15" oval or rectangular pan or oven proof dish (or a round one of equivalent area). Top evenly with meat.

- Sprinkle chopped chilies over bean and meat mixture, cover evenly with cheese. Drizzle with taco sauce. Cover and chill if made ahead.

- Bake in a 400° oven for 20 to 25 minutes or until very hot throughout. (Baking time may increase if nachos have been refrigerated.)

• • •

- Remove from oven and quickly garnish with some or all of the garnishes. Sprinkle green onions and ripe olives around the edges. Mound the avocado in the center, top with sour cream, the red pickled pepper and fresh cilantro sprigs.

- Quickly tuck the tortilla chips just around the edges of the bean mixture (making a petaled flower effect) and serve at once. If not serving at once, serve the chips separately so they won't get soggy.

- Scoop bean mixture with tortilla pieces, and, if desired, keep dish hot on an electric warming tray.

Note:This may also be served as a main dish along with a good Mexican salad of Romaine lettuce, sliced oranges, purple onion rings. Dress the salad with a good oil, vinegar, orange juice, salt, pepper and chili powder dressing. Serve an assortment of fresh fruit for dessert.

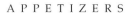
Armadillo Stew*

Serves 8 to 10

1 pound ground beef

1 pound ground pork

3 tablespoons bacon grease or olive oil

2 medium onions, chopped

1 bell pepper, chopped

1 clove garlic, crushed

2 large tomatoes, peeled and sliced

1½ tablespoons ground cumin seed

1 tablespoon brown sugar

1 tablespoon oregano

Salt and pepper to taste

1 10-ounce can crushed tomatoes

1 6-ounce can tomato paste

2 to 4 tablespoons chili powder

1 cup sliced pitted olives

¾ cup diced pimiento

¾ cup slivered almonds

¾ cup raisins

1 large can water chestnuts

6 cups Velveeta cheese

1 4-ounce can green chilies, diced

- Brown beef and pork, drain, set aside.

- Sauté onions, bell pepper, garlic. Add tomatoes, cumin seed, sugar, oregano, salt and pepper, canned tomatoes, tomato paste and chili powder. Cover, simmer 15 minutes. Add pimiento, raisins, olives, almonds, water chestnuts and green chilies. Simmer 15 more minutes. Add cheese and stir to melt.

- Serve on flour tortillas or as a dip with tortilla chips.

*Just teasing about the Armadillo.

Larry Vito's Jalapeño Dip

Makes about 2½ cups

1 16-ounce carton sour cream

½ cup finely chopped red onion

2 to 3 fresh jalapeño peppers, stemmed, seeded and finely chopped

1 tablespoon lemon juice

½ cup chopped fresh cilantro (or ½ cup chopped fresh parsley plus 1 teaspoon ground coriander)

½ teaspoon salt

¼ teaspoon freshly ground black pepper

- Combine all ingredients in small bowl. Cover and refrigerate several hours.

- To serve, bring to room temperature. Serve as a dip with toasted tortillas or toasted pita triangles. Also good as a topper for baked potatoes or potato pancakes.

Note: If the dip is too hot, cool it with low-fat plain yogurt.

Guacamole

Serves 8 to 10

3 or 4 large ripe avocados

1 bunch cilantro leaves (about 1 cup)

1 bunch scallions, diced (about 8)

Optionals:

2 fresh jalapeños seeded, deveined and diced

4 Oretega chilies, diced

Salt

- Mash avocados with a fork (do not use a food processor or blender). Combine with chopped cilantro leaves and the diced scallions.

• • •

- Add jalapeños or Ortega chilies and salt to taste. Serve with warm tortilla chips.

34

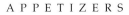

Hawaiian Guacamole

3 or 4 ripe avocados

¼ cup mango chutney, chop if too coarse

2 cloves garlic, minced

1 cup peeled, seeded, and chopped fresh tomatoes

1 lemon, juiced (or 2 limes, juiced)

Salt and pepper to taste

- Peel and seed the avocados. Mash with a fork. Combine with other ingredients. Guacamole should be lumpy. Chill and serve.

Herb Curry Dip

Makes 1½ cups

1 cup mayonnaise

½ cup sour cream

2 teaspoons minced mixed herbs (thyme, oregano, dill, tarragon)

¼ teaspoon salt

⅛ teaspoon curry powder

½ teaspoon Worcestershire sauce

1½ teaspoons lemon juice

1 tablespoon minced parsley

1 tablespoon grated onion

2 teaspoons rinsed and drained capers

- Blend all ingredients and chill well. Serve as a dip with raw vegetables.

Larry Vito's Red Hot White Bean Dip

Makes 2 cups

1 cup dried Great Northern, navy or pea beans, washed and picked over

½ cup olive oil

2 large cloves of garlic, finely chopped

1 teaspoon lemon juice

⅔ cup sour cream

1 teaspoon salt

½ teaspoon freshly ground black pepper

1 to 2 tablespoons liquid red-pepper seasoning

- Place beans in small, heavy saucepan; add enough cold water to cover the beans by 2 inches. Bring the beans and water to boiling over medium heat. Cover saucepan. Remove from heat and cool 1 hour.

- Return beans to medium heat; add cold water to cover beans by 2 inches. Bring to boiling, and reduce heat to simmer. Cover saucepan; simmer 1 to 1¼ hours until very soft. Check pan from time to time to make certain it is not boiling dry; if necessary, add a little more water. Drain beans well, reserving 3 table-spoons of cooking liquid.

- Place beans with the reserved cooking liquid in food processor. Purée. With motor running, add olive oil. Add garlic, lemon juice, sour cream, salt, pepper and 1 tablespoon liquid red-pepper seasoning. Taste and add the second tablespoon of liquid red-pepper sea-soning, if you wish.

- Purée until smooth and creamy. Cover and chill sev-eral hours to mellow flavors.

- To serve, bring to room temperature. Serve as a spread for crackers or as a dip for raw vegetables.

Variation: You can also add ½ cup chopped cilantro leaves and 1 to 2 chopped jalapeño peppers, seeded.

Spicy Pecans

3 tablespoons butter

2 teaspoons salt

2 tablespoons Worcestershire sauce

¼ teaspoon cayenne

½ teaspoon ground cinnamon

Tabasco - a good dash

1 pound shelled pecan halves

- Preheat oven to 300°.

- Melt butter in a large saucepan; remove from heat. Add seasonings and mix well. Gently toss in nuts.

- Place seasoned nuts in a single layer in a jelly roll pan. Bake at 300° for 25 to 30 minutes, turning frequently, until browned and crisp. Store tightly sealed in the refrigerator.

Rosemary Walnuts

6 tablespoons butter

1 tablespoon dried rosemary, crumbled

1 tablespoon salt

½ teaspoon cayenne

4 cups shelled walnut halves

- Preheat oven to 325°.

- Melt butter in large saucepan; remove from heat. Add seasonings and mix well. Gently toss in nuts.

- Place seasoned nuts in a single layer in a jelly roll pan. Bake at 325° for 10 to 15 minutes, stirring two or three times. Best when served warm.

Curried Peanuts and Cashews

3 tablespoons peanut oil

3 tablespoons curry powder

½ cup raw peanuts

½ cup raw cashews

- In a medium skillet, heat the peanut oil. Stir in curry powder and nuts. Stir and roast nuts until well coated and brown. Remove nuts to paper towel to drain. Serve warm.

"Honest bread is very well—it's the butter that makes the temptation."

Jerrold

A miniature tea service of Wedgwood makes a playful setting in the Children's Room.

Jefferson's Spoon Bread

Serves 4

4 cups milk

1 cup yellow cornmeal

¾ teaspoon salt

¾ tablespoon sugar

2 eggs

1 rounded tablespoon butter

- Place the milk in a double boiler and scald. Stir in the dry ingredients and continue to stir until thickened. Let cool 1 hour.

- Preheat oven to 400°.

- Beat eggs and stir into the cornmeal mixture with the butter. Place in a baking dish and bake for 30 minutes or until brown.

Blueberry Sally Lunn

Serves 8

2 cups sifted all-purpose flour

3 teaspoons baking powder

½ teaspoon salt

½ cup butter, softened

½ cup granulated sugar

2 eggs

¾ cup milk

1 cup blueberries, washed and drained

2 tablespoons light-brown sugar

½ teaspoon cinnamon

- Preheat oven to 375°. Grease and flour-dust an 8" x 8" x 2" pan. Sift flour, baking powder, salt. In large bowl of electric mixer, combine butter, granulated sugar and eggs; beat until fluffy.

- At low speed, add dry ingredients alternately with milk. Fold in blueberries. Turn into prepared pan; sprinkle with brown sugar and cinnamon.

- Bake about 35 minutes. Serve warm.

Note: If using frozen blueberries, do not thaw. Fold them into the batter while still frozen so they will not "bleed".

Oatmeal Crackers

About 3 dozen

2½ cups rolled oatmeal

½ cup cold water

Salt if desired

- Preheat oven to 275°.

- Stir 2 cups oatmeal together with the water until the dough holds together in a mass.

- Sprinkle a work surface with ¼ cup oatmeal, and place the dough on top. Use a rolling pin to roll dough to ⅛-inch thickness. To avoid sticking, move and lift dough as you roll it out, and sprinkle with more oatmeal. If dough cracks while you are rolling it, use your fingers to seal cracks. Trim edges to form a rectangle, roughly 10" x 7", and cut dough in half.

- Lift dough halves with a spatula, and place each on an ungreased cookie sheet. If desired, lightly sprinkle salt over the top. Score dough with a knife (do not cut through) into 1½-inch squares.

- Bake 30 minutes, turn over, and bake 15 to 20 minutes more. Edges of crackers will curl a bit; prevent this by occasionally pressing down edges with a metal spatula while baking.

- Remove from oven, cool on racks, and break into squares.

Boston Brown Bread

For centuries this has been a traditional New England Saturday night supper. In Puritan times no food was allowed to be cooked on Sunday, "The Sabbath." Hence, on Saturdays most ovens held a pot of beans baking and brown bread always accompanied.

Makes 2 loaves

1 cup unsifted whole wheat flour

1 cup unsifted rye flour

¾ cup yellow cornmeal

2 teaspoons baking soda

¼ teaspoon salt

2 large eggs, beaten (or ½ cup Egg Beaters)

1½ cups whole milk (or 1½ cups nonfat milk)

¾ cup dark molasses

1 cup dark seedless raisins

- Preheat oven to 350°. Grease and flour-dust two 1-pound coffee cans.

- In a large mixing bowl, thoroughly mix the flours, cornmeal, baking soda, salt, eggs (or Egg Beaters), milk, molasses and raisins.

- Pour batter into the prepared coffee cans. Bake in preheated oven for 1 hour and 10 to 15 minutes. Turn out onto wire racks to cool.

Note: The Egg Beaters and nonfat milk variations will provide a Brown Bread low in fats and cholesterol.

Oat Bran Muffins

Makes 12 muffins

1 cup wheat bran

1 cup oat bran

½ cup whole wheat flour

½ to ¾ cup white raisins

1 teaspoon baking soda

¼ teaspoon salt

½ cup honey

2 tablespoons safflower oil

1 egg

1 cup milk

- Preheat oven to 400°.

- In a large mixing bowl combine wheat bran, oat bran, whole wheat flour, white raisins, baking soda, salt, honey and safflower oil.

- In a separate bowl, beat well the egg and milk. Add this to the dry ingredients, stir to combine but do not overbeat.

- Spoon batter into greased or paper-lined muffin tins. Bake in preheated oven for 20 minutes.

Marjorie's Favorite Whole Wheat Rolls

Makes 36 rolls

½ **cup granulated sugar**

½ **cup shortening**

1 **teaspoon salt**

1 **cup boiling water**

2 **packages active dry yeast**

1 **teaspoon sugar**

1 **cup warm water**

1 **egg, beaten**

3 to 4 **cups unbleached white flour**

2 **cups whole wheat flour**

2 **cups graham cracker crumbs**

½ **cup (1 stick) butter, melted**

- Combine ½ cup sugar, ½ cup shortening, 1 teaspoon salt with 1 cup boiling water. Cool to lukewarm.

- Dissolve the yeast in 1 cup very warm water. Add 1 teaspoon sugar. Combine with the beaten egg and add to the shortening mixture.

- Sift 3 cups white flour with 2 cups whole wheat flour. Add to the other mixture and stir well; mixture will be stiff but sticky. Place in a mixing bowl and cover with plastic wrap; refrigerate overnight.

- The next day, punch down dough, and roll out to ¼-inch thick. Place graham cracker crumbs in one pie pan and melted butter in another. Cut dough into 2-inch round circles (using a 2-inch cookie cutter). Dip each roll first in melted butter and then in crumbs. With the back side of a table knife, crease each roll in the center, and fold over "Parker House Roll" style.

- Place rolls on a greased baking sheet, cover and let rise 1½ hours. When double in size, bake in a pre-heated 375° oven until lightly browned.

Note: These rolls are good slit open, buttered and toasted for breakfast as well as at lunch or dinner.

Sweet Oat Cornbread

Makes 1 loaf

⅓ **cup granulated sugar**

⅓ **cup butter, melted**

1 egg

2 cups milk

2 cups biscuit mix (baking mix)

1 cup cornmeal

½ **cup rolled oats**

1½ **teaspoons baking powder**

- Preheat oven to 375°.

- In a large bowl, beat together sugar, butter and egg. Gradually add milk, stirring until blended. Stir in baking mix, cornmeal, oats and baking powder until thoroughly combined. (Batter will be thin and runny.)

- Grease and flour-dust a 9" x 5" loaf pan. Pour batter into pan and bake in preheated oven for 45 to 50 minutes or until a toothpick inserted in the center comes out clean and crust is lightly browned. Cool on rack about 10 minutes, then turn out of the pan. Cut into thick slices and serve warm.

Note: If made ahead, cool completely, wrap in heavy foil, and refrigerate. To reheat, place bread (wrapped in foil) in a 350° oven until warm, about 30 to 35 minutes. Leftover slices can be toasted for breakfast or snacks.

Jalapeño Cornbread

Serves 8

- 1 cup yellow cornmeal
- 1 cup flour
- 1 tablespoon baking powder
- 2 jalapeños, seeded, deveined, and finely chopped
- ½ cup grated cheddar cheese
- 1 cup buttermilk
- 1 egg
- ¼ cup butter, melted

- Preheat oven to 400°.
- Combine cornmeal, flour, baking powder, jalapeños and Cheddar cheese in a bowl. Combine buttermilk, egg and butter and add to dry ingredients; stir until just mixed.
- Pour batter into a greased 8" x 8" x 2" baking pan. Bake in preheated oven for 30 minutes or until firm.

Maple Piñon Cornmeal Muffins

Makes 18

- 1¼ cups unbleached flour
- 1 cup yellow or blue cornmeal
- 1 teaspoon cinnamon
- 4 teaspoons baking powder
- ½ cup salt
- 1 cup coarsely ground piñon nuts (pine nuts), lightly toasted
- 1 stick unsalted butter, melted
- 1¼ cups half-and-half (light cream), warmed
- 2 extra large eggs
- 1 teaspoon vanilla
- 1 cup pure maple syrup

- Preheat oven to 400°.
- Combine dry ingredients and nuts, set aside. Beat eggs well, then add other wet ingredients (make sure the butter and cream are not too hot). Combine the liquid and dry ingredients, stirring just enough to produce a batter.
- Fill greased or papered muffin pans two-thirds full. Bake for 10 minutes, then rotate pans and bake another 4 minutes or until golden brown.

J. B.'s French Toast

This French Toast used to be served in the dining cars on the Santa Fe Railroad.

Serves 4

3 eggs

½ cup milk

½ teaspoon nutmeg

¼ teaspoon salt

2 cups cornflakes

4 tablespoons butter

6 slices dense white bread

6 tablespoons granulated sugar

- Stir the eggs, milk, nutmeg and salt together in a bowl until well blended. Strain the mixture through a sieve into a shallow bowl in which you can dip the bread easily (a soup bowl works well).

- Crumble the cornflakes slightly, making each flake about half its original size, and spread them on a piece of wax paper.

- Dip (don't soak) both sides of each slice of bread into the milk batter. Then press each slice of bread on both sides into the cornflakes to coat the bread well.

- Melt 2 tablespoons of the butter in a 12-inch skillet over medium heat and fry 3 slices of bread until golden on each side. When done, sprinkle about 1 tablespoon of sugar on top of each slice and keep warm in a 250° oven while you fry the other 3 slices in the remaining 2 tablespoons butter. Serve hot.

"My wife and I tried to breakfast together, but we had to stop or our marriage would have been wrecked."

Winston Churchill

Nanny's Biscuits

*This recipe is a favorite that comes from the culinary science and technique classes taught
throughout the country by Shirley Corriher from Atlanta, Georgia.*

Yields about 1 dozen

1½ **cups self-rising flour**

1 **teaspoon granulated sugar**

½ **teaspoon salt**

3 to 4 **tablespoons, shortening, cold**

¼ **teaspoon baking soda**

⅞ **cup buttermilk, cold**

- Preheat oven to 500°.

- In the work bowl of a food processor with the steel knife, combine the flour, salt, sugar and soda. Process a few seconds to blend.

- Add the shortening and process with a few on/offs until shortening is the size of small peas. Add the buttermilk. Process with 2 or 3 on/offs, just to mix. Dough should be wet. Do not overprocess. Permit dough to stand 2 to 5 minutes before shaping.

- To hand shape: In a shallow bowl, place some flour. Spoon a heaping tablespoon of wet dough into the flour, flour your fingers and sprinkle flour on the wet dough. Roll dough gently in the flour to coat well. Shape into a biscuit. Arrange the biscuits, touching each other, in a 9-inch cake pan.

- Let the shaped biscuits stand 10 minutes, then place on middle shelf of the preheated oven. Turn oven down to 475°. Bake 8 to 10 minutes.

Sponge Muffins

This is a very old fashioned recipe:
"Weight of the eggs in sugar. Half of the weight of eggs in flour. Juice and rind
of one lemon."

Makes 18

4 eggs, separated

1¼ cups granulated sugar

**1 lemon, grate the rind, squeeze the lemon juice
   (juice should measure about ¼ cup)**

¾ cup all-purpose flour

⅛ teaspoon salt

Powdered sugar

- Preheat oven to 350°.

- Beat egg yolks until lightened in color. Gradually add the granulated sugar, then add the lemon rind and juice. Continue beating until well blended.

- Beat egg whites until stiff but not dry. Fold the egg whites into the egg yolk mixture. Sift together the flour and salt; fold into the egg mixture.

- Grease and flour-dust 18 muffin tins. Spoon batter into prepared tins. Bake in preheated oven for 15 minutes. Remove to cooling racks and sprinkle with powdered sugar.

Papaya/Mango Coconut Bread

Makes 1 9-inch loaf

1 cup raisins

4 tablespoons rum or bourbon

½ cup unsalted butter, softened

½ cup granulated sugar

1 egg slightly beaten

⅓ cup milk

1 cup mashed papaya or mango (about 1 large papaya or mango)

2 cups all-purpose flour

1 teaspoon baking powder

1 teaspoon baking soda

½ teaspoon salt

1 cup unsweetened coconut flakes

- Preheat oven to 350°.

- In a small bowl, combine raisins and rum or bourbon and let stand at least 30 minutes, or up to several hours, stirring occasionally.

- In large mixing bowl, cream together butter and sugar until light and fluffy. Peel and pit the papaya or mango and crush in a small bowl with the back of a spoon. Add papaya, egg, milk and raisin mixture to the butter and sugar mixture.

- In separate, medium bowl, sift together flour, baking powder, baking soda and salt. Stir in coconut. Mix dry ingredients into wet ingredients, beating until batter is thoroughly blended.

- Spread mixture evenly in a greased 9-inch loaf pan and bake for 1 hour or until cake tester inserted in center comes out clean. Cool 5 minutes in pan on rack and then turn out on rack to cool completely.

Raspberry Nut Bread

**Makes one 9" x 5" x 3" loaf or
five 4½" x 2¾" x 2½" loaves**

1 cup butter

1½ cups granulated sugar

1 teaspoon vanilla

¼ teaspoon lemon extract

4 eggs

3 cups all-purpose flour, sifted

1 teaspoon salt

1 teaspoon cream of tartar

½ teaspoon baking soda

1 cup raspberry jam

½ cup dairy sour cream

1 cup broken pecans

- Preheat oven to 350°.

- In mixing bowl cream butter, sugar, vanilla and lemon extract until fluffy. Add eggs one at a time, beating well after each addition.

- Sift together flour, salt, cream of tartar and soda. Combine jam and sour cream, add jam mixture and dry mixture alternately to butter mixture. Beat well until combined. Stir in nuts.

- Grease and flour-dust the loaf pan or pans. Pour batter into prepared pans and bake in preheated oven for 55 minutes. Cool 20 minutes in pan. Remove from pans and cool completely on wire racks. Slice carefully.

Note: If using smaller pans, adjust baking time accordingly.

Almond Raisin Bread

Makes 1 loaf

½ cup brown sugar

¾ cup hot water

½ cup molasses

¾ cup half-and-half, or milk

1 cup flour

3 teaspoons baking powder

1 teaspoon salt

½ teaspoon baking soda

2 cups graham flour

1 tablespoon butter, melted

¼ cup raisins, chopped

1 cup almonds, chopped

- Preheat oven to 350°.

- In a large mixing bowl, combine the brown sugar and hot water. Stir until the sugar is dissolved. Add the molasses and the half-and-half, or milk. Blend well.

- In a separate bowl, sift together the flour, baking powder, salt and baking soda. Stir dry ingredients into the milk mixture. Add the graham flour, melted butter, raisins and almonds. Blend everything thoroughly.

- Pour batter into a well-buttered loaf pan. Bake in preheated oven for 1½ hours.

Orange Bread

Makes 2 loaves

6 tablespoons orange peel

Light corn syrup

1¼ cups granulated sugar

1 teaspoon salt

3½ cups sifted pastry flour

3 teaspoons baking powder

1 egg, beaten

1⅜ cups milk

3 tablespoons melted shortening

- Peel orange removing only the outer yellow rind. Cut rind into strips. Drop into a pan with the light corn syrup. Bring to a simmer and remove from heat. Let stand 24 hours before using. Next day, heat the syrup and drain orange rind. Chop coarsely.

- Preheat oven to 350°.

- Sift dry ingredients together. Combine beaten egg, milk, melted shortening and orange peel. Combine the 2 mixtures and stir until batter is smooth. Pour into 2 greased loaf pans. Let stand 20 minutes.

- Bake in moderate oven, 350°, about 30 minutes.

Peanut Bread

Makes 2 loaves

1 cup sifted all-purpose flour

1 teaspoon baking powder

1¼ teaspoons soda

1 teaspoon salt

⅓ cup granulated sugar

2 cups whole wheat flour

1 cup raw peanuts, chopped

½ cup raisins, chopped

2 cups buttermilk

⅓ cup molasses

7 teaspoons water

- Preheat oven to 350°.

- Sift together flour, baking powder, soda, salt and sugar. Stir in whole wheat flour. Add nuts and raisins.

- Combine buttermilk, molasses and water. Add liquid ingredients to dry mixture. Stir just enough to moisten dry ingredients. Turn into 2 greased loaf pans. Bake in 350° oven for about 1 hour.

Molasses and Ginger Scones

Makes 6 large scones

1⅞ cups whole wheat flour

2 tablespoons brown sugar-firmly packed

½ teaspoon baking soda

1 tablespoon baking powder

Pinch of salt

½ teaspoon ground ginger

4 tablespoons butter, cut into bits

1 large egg, beaten

2 tablespoons molasses

½ cup lowfat yogurt

¼ cup raisins, or currants

- Preheat oven to 425°.

- Using a wooden spoon, combine the first 6 ingredients. Then add the remaining ingredients in the order listed, stir until very thick.

- Turn the dough onto a floured surface, form a ball and knead until it holds together. Add flour if dough is too sticky, but the dough should be slightly tacky.

- Pat ball down to ½-inch thickness and, using a 4 or 5 inch heart-shaped cookie cutter, cut the hearts from it. Place the scones on a cookie sheet and bake in the preheated oven for 15 minutes, or until golden brown and firm to the touch. Serve with your favorite jam.

*"Noncooks think it's silly to
invest two hours work in
two minutes enjoyment, but
if cooking is evanescent,
well, so is the ballet."*

Julia Child

Soups

The Dining Room of Kenmore.
This splendid room is included in Helen Comstock's **The 100 Most
Beautiful Rooms in America**. It is arranged according to the descrip-
tion of the 1782 inventory. The Chippendale-style banquet table in
three parts was made in nearby Spotsylvania County, ca. 1775, and is
set for a magnificent dessert course.

Frozen Tomato Soup

Serves 8

4 cups peeled, seeded and chopped tomatoes
   (about 4 pounds)

1 cup chopped white onion

½ cup white wine vinegar

1½ teaspoons salt

¾ teaspoon white pepper

- Peel, seed and chop tomatoes. Combine tomatoes with onion, vinegar, salt and pepper in a blender or food processor. Purée until smooth.

- Pour tomato purée into a non-aluminum container (the tomato and vinegar acids may react with aluminum) and place in freezer. Freeze for 3 to 4 hours, stirring often to break up ice crystals.

- Serve in glass dishes. The "soup" should be mushy as a sorbet.

Note: This soup lends itself very well to flavors of fresh herbs. Two or three teaspoons of freshly minced oregano, basil or tarragon can be added for stronger flavor.

Cold Tomato Lime Soup

Serves 6

1 tablespoon butter

1 large onion, chopped

2 tablespoons chopped scallions

6 large tomatoes, peeled, seeded and chopped

2 cups chicken broth

1 tablespoon tomato paste

2 teaspoons fresh thyme (1 teaspoon dried)

1 teaspoon granulated sugar

1 cup heavy cream

6 tablespoons lime juice, freshly squeezed

Dash of liquid red pepper seasoning

Garnish:

⅓ cup sour cream

Chopped chives

Thin lime slices

- Melt butter in a large saucepan. Add onion and scallions and place a round of buttered wax paper directly onto onion mixture. Cook over low heat for 15 minutes.

- Remove wax paper, stir in tomatoes, chicken broth, tomato paste, thyme, sugar, salt and pepper. Increase heat to medium and simmer 20 minutes. Remove from heat and cool.

- In blender or food processor, purée the tomato mixture until smooth. Add heavy cream, lime juice and liquid red pepper seasoning. Cover and chill until serving time.

• • •

- Garnish cold soup with dollops of sour cream, sprinkle with chopped chives and twist a lime slice on the edge of the bowl.

Note: If soup remains too thick, thin with additional cream or chicken broth.

Chilled Stilton and Pear Soup

Serves 8

1 tablespoon vegetable oil

6 tablespoons unsalted butter

1 tablespoon water

½ cup all-purpose flour

2 stalks celery, chopped

¼ pound Monterey Jack cheese, grated

1 medium onion, chopped

1 medium leek, white part only, chopped

1 tablespoon fresh lemon juice

2 small pears, unpeeled

Salt and pepper to season

½ cup half-and-half

6 cups chicken stock

6 ounces Stilton cheese, broken into 2-inch pieces

- Heat vegetable oil and water, add celery, onion and leek. Season with salt and pepper and sauté until onions are translucent. Add stock and simmer for 15 minutes.

- To make a roux, melt butter and add flour, stir continually for 6 to 8 minutes. Strain 4 cups simmering stock into the roux, whisk until smooth. Combine with remaining stock and vegetables. Simmer an additional 15 minutes. Remove from heat and whisk in grated cheese, 1 cup at a time. Strain the soup and cool in an ice water bath.

- Acidulate, with lemon juice, 4 cups water. Core and medium dice unpeeled pears and immediately place in acidulated water. Strain and rinse pears under cold running water, drain well and add to soup with half-and-half and Stilton cheese. Refrigerate for 2 hours before serving.

Note: This soup is best eaten on the day of preparation. If pears are unavailable you may substitute a good, sweet apple. If soup is not served on the same day as prepared do not add diced fruit until shortly before serving.

Curried Tomato Bisque

Serves 10 to 12

2 tablespoons butter

1½ cups chopped onions

1½ cloves garlic, minced

1 to 2 tablespoons curry powder

5 cups peeled, cored and quartered ripe tomatoes (about 2½ pounds) (canned Italian plum tomatoes may be substituted)

½ bay leaf

1 teaspoon chopped fresh thyme (½ teaspoon dried)

½ cup uncooked rice

2 cups homemade chicken stock

⅛ teaspoon liquid red pepper seasoning

1½ teaspoons salt

2 cups milk

1 cup heavy cream

- In a large pot, melt the butter and sauté the onions and garlic until wilted. Sprinkle with curry and cook for 3 minutes, stirring often.

- Peel, core, and quarter the tomatoes. To the onion mixture, add the tomatoes, bay leaf, thyme, rice, stock, liquid red pepper seasoning and salt. Cover and simmer 45 minutes, stirring occasionally.

- Remove bay leaf and purée tomato mixture. Add milk and cream, blend well. This bisque may be served either hot or cold.

Cream of California Herbs

Serves 6

4 cups homemade chicken stock

3 tablespoons uncooked rice

2 cups chopped lettuce leaves

¼ cup finely chopped fresh parsley or chervil

¼ cup finely chopped shallots or scallions

1 teaspoon finely minced fresh tarragon

1 teaspoon finely minced fresh rosemary

3 or 4 spinach leaves

2 teaspoons prepared horseradish

1 teaspoon fresh-squeezed lemon juice

Salt and pepper

1 cup heavy cream

3 egg yolks

Chives, minced for garnish

- Bring chicken stock to a boil and add rice. Cook 10 minutes. Add lettuce, parsley or chervil, shallots or scallions, tarragon and rosemary. Cook 10 minutes more. Put in blender and blend until smooth. (Depending on your blender, you may want to do this in batches.)

- Add spinach leaves to the blender and purée. Add horseradish and lemon juice. Salt and pepper to taste.

- Combine the cream and egg yolks, blend thoroughly. Add to the herb mixture. Serve hot or cold topped with minced chives.

Variation: This soup can be extended by adding 4 sliced zucchinis and 1 cup of green peas to the simmering mixture.

Cauliflower and Leek Vichyssoise with Cardamon

Serves 6 to 8

1 large cauliflower (2½ pounds), coarsely chopped (trim and reserve 8 florets for garnish)

2 tablespoons olive oil

1 large garlic clove, minced

1 medium jalapeño chili, seeded and minced

2 medium onions, coarsely chopped

1 medium leek, white part only, rinsed thoroughly and coarsely chopped

½ teaspoon ground cardamon

⅛ teaspoon ground mace

4½ cups chicken stock, preferably homemade

2 teaspoons salt, or to taste

- Bring 1 quart of water to boil. Add the 8 cauliflower florets and cook until just tender, about 4 minutes. Remove the florets from the water and place in a bowl of ice water to stop the cooking process. Drain and set aside.

- In a large, 4-quart saucepan, heat the olive oil and add the next 6 ingredients. Sauté until the vegetables soften, about 5 minutes. Add the chopped cauliflower and the stock. Bring to a boil, cover, and reduce heat to a simmer. Cook until vegetables are tender, about 25 minutes.

- Purée the soup in batches in a food processor or blender. Season with salt.

- The soup can be served warm or cold. Garnish with the reserved cauliflower florets.

Okra Soup

Serves 6

4 cups thinly sliced okra

¼ cup butter

4 cups chicken or veal stock

- In a large skillet, cook the okra in the butter for 15 minutes, stirring constantly "until the goo runs." Do not brown.

- In a saucepan, heat the stock to a boil. Add the okra and boil over medium heat until the okra is soft and almost falling apart. Season with salt and pepper. Serve hot.

Creamy Carrot Soup

Serves 4

2¾ cups homemade chicken stock

1 pound carrots, peeled and sliced

1 medium onion, coarsely chopped

1½ teaspoons curry powder

1 teaspoon chopped fresh thyme (½ teaspoon dried thyme)

½ teaspoon freshly grated nutmeg

1 clove garlic, minced

1 bay leaf

1 cup milk

3 ounces cream cheese, cubed

1 teaspoon grated orange peel

Salt to taste

Garnish:
Sliced almonds

Minced parsley

- In a large saucepan over medium heat, combine chicken stock, carrots, onion, curry powder, thyme, nutmeg, garlic and bay leaf. Cover and simmer until vegetables are tender, about 15 minutes. Discard bay leaf. Purée the soup in a blender or food processor in 4 batches. (This can be done as much as 8 hours ahead.)

- Return soup to saucepan. Stir in milk. Warm gently over low heat until thoroughly heated. Add cream cheese and stir until melted. Blend in orange peel and salt to taste.

• • •

- In a small skillet, toast the sliced almonds to a delicate brown color. Use the almonds and parsley as a garnish for the soup.

Yellow Bell Pepper Soup

Serves 4

2 tablespoons butter

3 yellow bell peppers, coarsely chopped

2 leeks, chopped

1 onion, chopped

2 celery ribs, chopped

4 cups homemade chicken stock

- In a large saucepan, melt butter, add yellow pepper, leek, onion and celery. Sauté covered for 15 minutes.

- Add chicken stock and bring to a boil. Lower heat to a simmer and continue cooking for 45 minutes. Pour soup into a blender and purée until smooth.

Note: This soup lends itself to a garnish of freshly minced oregano and/or basil and a drizzle of olive oil at serving time.

Oven Fish Chowder

Serves 8

2 pounds boneless cod or haddock fillets (or other firm-fleshed fish)

4 potatoes, peeled and sliced

2 tablespoons chopped celery leaves

1 bay leaf

1 tablespoon salt

4 whole cloves

1 clove garlic, minced

½ cup butter

¼ teaspoon dill seed

¼ teaspoon white pepper

½ cup white wine or Vermouth

2 cups boiling water

2 cups half-and-half (light cream)

2 tablespoons chopped fresh dill

2 tablespoons chopped fresh parsley

- Preheat oven to 375°.

- Into a large ovenproof casserole, place the fish fillets, potatoes, celery leaves, bay leaf, salt, cloves, garlic, butter, dill seed, white pepper, white wine and water. Cover and bake for 1 hour.

- Heat cream to the scalding point and add just before serving. Stir to break up the fish fillets.

- Garnish each chowder dish with a sprinkling of freshly chopped dill and parsley.

Louisiana Crab, Corn and Shrimp Bisque

Serves 6

2 pounds unshelled raw shrimp

1 small onion, quartered

½ lemon, sliced

6 black peppercorns

¼ cup dry white wine or Vermouth

3 cups water

1 small onion, chopped

1 rib celery, chopped

3 scallions, chopped

3 tablespoons chopped parsley

3 cloves garlic, chopped

¼ red bell pepper, chopped

¼ green bell pepper, chopped

3 ears of corn, kernels to measure 1½ cups

¼ cup vegetable oil

¼ cup flour

4 tablespoons butter, softened

½ cup dry white wine or Vermouth

1 teaspoon fresh thyme (½ teaspoon dried)

3½ cups heavy cream

1 teaspoon liquid red pepper seasoning

Salt and pepper

½ pound fresh lump crabmeat

16 crab claws, cooked and shelled, for garnish (optional)

- The shrimp stock: Remove shells from the shrimp and set aside the shrimp. In a large pot combine the shrimp shells, quartered onion, lemon slices, peppercorns, white wine and water. Bring to a boil, reduce heat and simmer for 20 minutes. Strain.

- In a large saucepan combine onion, celery, scallions, parsley, garlic, red and green peppers and corn kernels in the vegetable oil and sauté until just tender. Add the shrimp stock (which should measure about 3 cups) and simmer for 20 to 30 minutes, or until corn is tender.

- Knead flour and butter together. Remove 1½ cups of the shrimp stock to a small saucepan, whisk the flour-butter mixture into the stock. Return this thickened stock to the larger saucepan and stir to combine.

- Add the white wine, thyme, cream and liquid red pepper seasoning. Season with salt and pepper if needed. Just before serving add the reserved shrimp and the lump crabmeat, simmer just until shrimp and crab turn pink and are cooked. (Do not overcook the shrimp or it will toughen.) Ladle bisque into heated soup bowls and garnish with crab claws if desired.

French Mushroom Soup

Serves 12

½ **cup minced onion**

½ **cup unsalted butter**

6 **tablespoons flour**

12 **cups rich, homemade chicken broth**

2 **sprigs parsley**

½ **bay leaf**

½ **teaspoon fresh thyme (¼ teaspoon dried)**

2 **pounds fresh mushrooms, thinly sliced**

8 **ounces dried imported mushrooms, such as Chanterelles, Morels or Porcini**

1 **cup warm water**

½ **teaspoon salt**

1 **teaspoon lemon juice**

1 **cup whipping cream**

¾ **cup chopped fresh parsley**

- Cook onions in 4 tablespoons butter until soft. Stir in the flour and cook over low heat for 4 minutes without browning. Add the broth, blending thoroughly with the flour.

- Add the parsley, bay leaf and thyme and simmer for 20 minutes.

- Soak the dried mushrooms in warm water for 20 minutes. Lift mushrooms out of the water and wash thoroughly to remove any sand and grit. Chop mushrooms coarsely. Strain the mushroom liquid through a coffee filter and set aside.

- Melt the remaining butter in a skillet, add the fresh and the reconstituted mushrooms. Toss with salt and lemon juice.

- Add the mushrooms and the reserved mushroom liquid to the soup broth and simmer 5 minutes. If not to be used immediately, set aside.

- Reheat the soup to a simmer. Add the cream and just warm through. Taste for seasoning, adding salt and pepper if needed. Serve immediately, garnish with chopped parsley.

Swiss Barley Soup

Serves 6 to 8

3 strips lean bacon

3 ounces smoked ham, finely diced

1 medium onion, peeled and diced

1 small leek, white part only, finely diced

1 small rib of celery, finely diced

¾ cup barley, uncooked

10 cups rich homemade chicken broth

Salt

Freshly ground white pepper

Freshly grated nutmeg

1 cup half-and-half

½ teaspoon Maggi

1 tablespoon chopped fresh parsley

- In a 5-quart heavy saucepan with lid, sauté the bacon over medium heat until most of the fat is melted but the bacon has not browned. Add the diced ham, onion, leek, celery and the barley; cook, stirring occasionally, for 3 minutes. Pour in the chicken broth and bring to a boil. Reduce heat, partially cover saucepan, and simmer for 1½ hours, stirring occasionally.

- Add the half-and-half and simmer 30 minutes more. Season with Maggi, salt, pepper and nutmeg. Stir in chopped parsley and serve.

Corned Beef and Cabbage Soup

Serves 4

1 small head savoy or green cabbage

1 clove garlic

6 tablespoons butter, approximately

½ teaspoon fresh thyme leaves (¼ teaspoon dried)

1½ tablespoons caraway seeds, optional

Salt and pepper

1 quart homemade chicken stock

½ cup beer (optional)

¾ cup shredded Swiss cheese (about ¼ pound)

¾ pound thick-sliced corned beef

1 loaf crusty Italian bread

- Remove the outer layers of dark cabbage leaves. Quarter, core, and slice the head into thin, short shreds. Mince the garlic.

- Melt 4 tablespoons of the butter in a large pot and stir in the cabbage, garlic, thyme, caraway seeds and about ½ teaspoon salt. Cook over medium-high heat stirring frequently, until cabbage is wilted, about 5 minutes. Add the stock and beer and bring to a simmer. Cook until cabbage is very tender, about 30 minutes.

- Shred the cheese and cut the corned beef into julienne slices.

- Preheat the broiler. Cut eight ¼-inch thick slices of bread. Melt remaining 2 tablespoons butter and brush on both sides of each slice of bread. Put on a baking sheet and toast in preheated broiler just until golden on each side. Top slices with cheese and return to broiler until cheese is melted. Watch carefully so it does not burn.

- Reheat soup if necessary. Add the corned beef to the soup. Just heat through and season to taste with salt and pepper. At the last moment, top the soup with the cheese croutons. Pass extra croutons as needed.

Hot Garlic Sopa

Serves 4

¼ cup olive oil

4 large cloves garlic, minced

4 corn tortillas, cut in sixths (or 1 cup tortilla chips, broken pieces will be acceptable)

4 cups homemade beef broth

1 or more large fresh New Mexico hot green chilies, peeled, seeded, chopped (if fresh chilies are unavailable, substitute pickled jalapeños)

2 teaspoons ground pure New Mexico hot red chili

4 eggs

1 cup grated Monterey Jack cheese

2 tablespoons finely minced fresh or pickled jalapeño peppers

- Heat oil in 3-quart saucepan with close fitting lid. Add garlic and cook briefly; then add tortilla pieces or chips and cook until lightly browned, crushing chips with back of wooden spoon. Stir in broth, green chilies and 1 teaspoon ground chili. Bring to a simmer. Meanwhile preheat oven to 450°.

- Break 1 egg into a small bowl. Stir soup rapidly in a small circle, then slide egg into center of circle. Repeat with remaining 3 eggs, working quickly. Cover 2 to 3 minutes to soft poach. Set 4 heated oven proof bowls on a baking sheet. Spoon soup into bowls, placing 1 poached egg in center of each bowl. Sprinkle with ¼ cup cheese. Set in oven just until cheese is melted. Sprinkle each bowl of soup with ¼ teaspoon ground chili.

- Depending on your guests' tastes, either top each serving with 1½ teaspoons minced jalapeños or serve jalapeños separately, to be added to taste.

"Garlic is the catsup of intellectuals."

Unknown

Lisa's Green Chili Soup

Serves 8

2 tablespoons vegetable oil

1 pound poblano or Anaheim chilies, roasted, peeled, seeded and chopped, or 2 cans (7 ounces each) roasted, peeled California chilies, drained

1 small onion, chopped

8 cups chicken stock, preferably homemade

4 skinless, boneless chicken breast halves

1 sprig (4 or 5 leaves) fresh epazote, minced, or ¼ teaspoon dried (see Note: optional)

½ teaspoon salt

¼ teaspoon pepper

4 corn tortillas, cut into ¼-inch squares

4 cups corn kernels (from 6 to 8 ears of corn) or 3 packages (10 ounces each) frozen, thawed

1 pound Monterey Jack cheese, cut into ¼-inch dice

Sour cream

- Preheat the oven to 300°. In a medium skillet, heat the oil. Add the chilies and the onion and sauté over moderately high heat until tender, about 5 minutes. Scrape the mixture into a food processor or a blender and purée. Set aside.

- In a large saucepan, bring the stock to a boil over high heat. Reduce the heat to a simmer and add the chicken. Poach until tender and no longer pink in the center, about 15 minutes. Remove the chicken and let stand until cool enough to handle. Shred the chicken and return it to the stock. Add the puréed chilies, the epazote, salt and pepper and simmer gently for 30 minutes.

- Meanwhile, spread out the tortilla squares on a large baking sheet. Bake for about 15 minutes, until brown. (These crunchy garnishes are called totopos.)

- In a blender or food processor, purée 2 cups of the corn with 2 cups of the soup stock. Add to the soup along with the remaining 2 cups whole corn kernels. Simmer until tender, about 5 minutes.

- To serve, put about ¼ cup of the diced Monterey Jack cheese into each bowl. Ladle in the hot chili soup. Top with a spoonful of sour cream and a sprinkling of totopos.

Note: Epazote is a mild Mexican herb available at Latin American groceries and some spice shops. It grows easily in home herb gardens.

Texas Black Bean and Jalapeño Jack Cheese Soups
with Smoked Red and Yellow Pepper Creams

This soup is presented with the black bean and cheese soups in the same bowl, similar to the Yin-Yang Chinese soups. The smoked red and yellow pepper creams are drizzled over the top. This recipe is served at The Mansion on Turtle Creek, Dallas, Texas.

Serves 6

Black Bean Soup

1 cup dry black beans

1 onion, chopped

3 cloves garlic, chopped

1 jalapeño chili, seeded and chopped

1 small leek, white part only, chopped

1 rib celery, chopped

4 sprigs fresh cilantro

4 cups homemade chicken stock

1 cup ham scraps or 1 large ham bone

Salt to taste

Ground black pepper to taste

¼ cup lemon juice, freshly squeezed

- Rinse beans and discard any that are shriveled. Soak beans in cold water to cover for 2 to 3 hours; drain.

- Place soaked beans, onion, garlic, chili, leek, celery, cilantro, chicken stock and ham (or ham bone) in a large stock pot and bring to a boil over high heat. Lower heat and simmer for about 2 hours or until beans are very soft, skimming off foam frequently.

- When beans are soft, remove ham scraps or bone. Pour beans into a blender or food processor and blend until smooth. Strain and season to taste with salt, pepper and lemon juice. Soup should be thick, but if it is too thick, thin with additional hot chicken stock.

Continued on next page

Jalapeño Jack Cheese Soup

2 tablespoons vegetable oil

1 onion, chopped

1 small leek, white part only, chopped

1 rib celery, chopped

2 cloves garlic, chopped

1½ cups flat beer

½ cup white wine

4 cups homemade chicken stock

1 jalapeño chili, seeded and chopped

Herb bouquet: 1 bay leaf, 5 sprigs fresh thyme and 1 tablespoon white peppercorns tied in cheesecloth bag.

2 tablespoons softened unsalted butter

2 tablespoons flour

1 cup shredded jalapeño Jack cheese

¼ cup heavy cream

Salt to taste

Ground black pepper to taste

¼ cup freshly squeezed lemon juice

• Heat oil in a large sauté pan over medium heat. Sauté onion, leek, celery and garlic for about 5 minutes or until soft. Add beer and wine and bring to a boil. Cook for about 10 minutes or until liquid is reduced by half.

• Add chicken stock, jalapeño chili and herb bouquet. Bring to a boil. Skim foam from top, lower heat, and simmer for about 1 hour. Remove bouquet.

• Knead together butter and flour. Slowly whisk into soup and blend until smooth. Simmer for an additional 30 minutes. Remove from heat and immediately stir in cheese and heavy cream and blend with whisk until smooth.

• Place liquid in blender or food processor and blend until smooth. Strain and season to taste with salt, pepper and lemon juice. Soup should be very thick, but if it is too thick, thin with additional hot chicken stock.

Continued on next page

Smoked Red and Yellow Pepper Creams

1 red bell pepper

¼ cup very cold heavy cream

½ cup sour cream

Salt to taste

Lime juice to taste

1 yellow bell pepper

Liquid smoke seasoning to taste (or mesquite seasoning)

- Roast and peel the bell peppers.

- To make the Red Pepper Cream: Using a food processor or a blender, purée the pepper until very smooth. Add 2 tablespoons cream and ¼ cup sour cream. Add 2 to 4 drops of liquid smoke seasoning. Process briefly to combine. Season to taste with salt and lime juice. Strain through a fine sieve.

- Pour the cream into a catsup-like squeeze bottle and set aside.

- Clean the bowl of the food processor or blender and repeat the process using the yellow pepper and the remaining ingredients. Pour into another squeeze bottle and set aside.

Advance Preparation:
- Soups may be prepared up to 1 day ahead and refrigerated. Reheat and adjust seasoning and thickness just before serving.

- Smoke creams may be prepared several hours ahead and refrigerated until ready to use.

Serving:
Warm soup plates and simultaneously pour ladlesful of hot Black Bean Soup and Jalapeño Jack Cheese Soup into the soup plates. Pour gently so that soups meet in the center of the soup plates but do not mix.

Using the squeeze bottles, streak the Red Pepper Cream over the surface of the Jalapeño Jack Soup and the Yellow Pepper Cream over the surface of the Black Bean Soup. The effect should be similar to a modern painting. Serve immediately.

Southwestern Peanut Soup

Serves 6

¼ **cup butter**

¼ **cup minced onion**

¼ **cup chopped celery**

1 **cup creamy peanut butter**

1 **tablespoon flour**

4 **cups homemade beef or veal broth**

2 **teaspoons lemon juice**

½ **cup Spanish peanuts, chopped**

- In the top part of a double boiler, melt butter. Add onion and celery; sauté until tender. Place over boiling water. Add peanut butter and flour; blend well. Stir in broth and lemon juice. Cook 20 minutes, stirring occasionally.

- At serving time, garnish with chopped Spanish peanuts.

Cream of Almond Soup

Serves 4

2 **tablespoons butter**

1 **rib celery, minced**

1 **clove garlic, crushed**

3 **cups homemade chicken broth**

⅔ **cup ground blanched almonds**

Dash of mace

1 **cup heavy cream**

2 **tablespoons dry sherry**

Salt

½ **cup sliced almonds, toasted**

- In a heavy saucepan sauté celery and garlic in butter for 4 or 5 minutes. Add chicken broth, ground blanched almonds and mace. Cover and simmer 30 minutes, stirring occasionally. Remove from heat. Cool.

- Purée soup in blender at low speed or press through a fine sieve. Return mixture to saucepan. Stir in 1 cup heavy cream. Heat, uncovered, stirring occasionally for 2 to 3 minutes. Add 2 tablespoons of sherry. Do not boil. Season with salt if necessary. Ladle into bowls and sprinkle with toasted almonds.

Hearty Duck and Wild Rice Soup

Serves 6 or more

1 5-pound duck, preferably fresh

Salt to taste

Freshly ground pepper

1 onion (about ½ pound), coarsely chopped

1 carrot, coarsely chopped

1 clove garlic, thinly sliced

10 cups rich homemade chicken broth (see note)

1 cup mushrooms, preferably shitake or other
  wild domestic mushrooms

2 cups cooked wild rice

1 cup finely minced leeks

1 cup finely diced carrots

Note: If you wish, you may use duck broth made with carcasses of leftover cooked duck.

- Cut duck into serving pieces. Crack the backbone in half lenthwise. Cut away and discard any peripheral fat from the duck pieces. Sprinkle the pieces with salt and pepper.

- Heat a heavy kettle and add the duck pieces skin side down. Add as many pieces in one layer as the kettle will hold. Cook these pieces until they are nicely browned. As the pieces are cooked, strain off and discard the fat.

- Return all the pieces to the kettle and add the onion, carrot and garlic; cook 3 minutes stirring constantly.

- Add the broth and bring to a boil. Simmer about 1 hour or until the liquid is reduced to about 6 cups. Skim off any scum and fat from the top as it accumulates.

- Remove and reserve the meaty duck pieces, such as legs, breasts and thighs. Discard the boney parts such as the backbone.

- Strain the 6 cups of duck soup into a saucepan and bring to a simmer.

- Remove the meat from the reserved duck pieces and cut it into small dice. There should be about 2 cups.

- Cut the mushrooms into small squares. There should be about 2 cups.

- Put the mushrooms, diced meat, wild rice, leeks and carrots into a kettle and pour the hot soup over them. Let simmer about 2 minutes. Serve piping hot.

75

Curried Wild Turkey Soup

Serves 6

1 turkey carcass

1 celery rib, chopped

1 carrot, chopped

1 onion, chopped

1 bay leaf

6 cups rich turkey stock

1 cup chopped onion

1 cup peeled and roughly chopped Granny Smith apples

½ teaspoon salt

¼ teaspoon cardamon

2 teaspoons curry powder

3 egg yolks

1 cup buttermilk

¼ teaspoon garlic powder

1 cup cubed cooked turkey

Garnishes:

½ cup minced parsley

6 strips bacon, cooked and crumbled

½ cup blanched almonds sautéed in butter

- Make the turkey stock by sawing the carcass, if you need to, to fit in a large pot. Fill the pot with cold water until it covers the bones. Add the celery, carrot, onion and bay leaf. Bring to a boil, reduce heat and simmer for 3 to 4 hours, until the bones fall apart. Cool, discard the bones and any skin and measure out 6 cups of stock. (If you have a lot of stock, boil it to reduce it to 6 cups. This will intensify the flavors.)

- Simmer the stock with the onion, apples, cardamon, curry and salt for 30 minutes. Purée in blender or food processor.

- Beat egg yolks, garlic powder and buttermilk together and add to the stock with the cubed turkey. Heat just to the boiling point. Do not allow to boil.

•   •   •

- Serve in heated bowls and garnish with parsley, bacon bits and almonds.

Note: If you have no luck in the woods with a wild turkey, a domestic turkey will do very nicely.

Creamy Wild Rice Soup

The origin of this recipe is credited to the Marquette Hotel in Minneapolis, Minnesota,
the state most famous for growing wild rice.

Serves 6

2 tablespoons butter

⅓ cup raw wild rice (yields 2 cups cooked)

2 tablespoons sliced almonds

½ cup finely chopped onions

½ cup finely chopped carrots

¼ cup finely chopped celery

4 cups homemade chicken stock

2 teaspoons arrowroot (or as needed)

2 cups heavy cream

- Melt butter in a large saucepan, add rice, almonds, onions, carrots and celery. Sauté for about 8 minutes until the vegetables are softened. Add the stock to the saucepan and bring to a boil, then lower heat to a simmer for about 1 hour, uncovered.

- Check the consistency of the soup. It should have body and not be too watery. If necessary, thicken with 2 teaspoons arrowroot dissolved in ¼ cup heavy cream. Stir the remaining cream into the soup and reheat before serving. (Do not allow soup to boil after cream has been added.)

New Age Albondegas Soup

Serves 4 to 6

1½ pounds ground turkey

2 tablespoons minced parsley

2 teaspoons ground cumin

1 tablespoon paprika

Few dashes cayenne pepper (optional)

1½ teaspoons sea salt (optional)

3 tablespoons vegetable oil

4 cups tomato juice

4 cups chicken broth

1 large onion, chopped

1 large carrot, thinly sliced

1 large celery rib, thinly sliced

1 red bell pepper, sliced

1 green bell pepper, sliced

1 yellow bell pepper, sliced

1 large potato, peeled and diced

1 large tomato, chopped

Freshly ground black pepper, to taste (optional)

Sea salt, to taste (optional)

1 cup chopped cilantro leaves

½ cup thinly sliced scallions, for garnish

Yellow or blue corn tortilla chips

- Place the first 6 ingredients in a large bowl, and mix together well with your hands. Form into 1-inch balls.

- In a large skillet over high heat, heat the vegetable oil and cook the turkey until lightly browned on all sides. (Cook a few at a time, and do not crowd the pan.) Remove from the heat, and set aside.

- In a large soup pot, place the next 12 ingredients. Add the meatballs, and simmer for 30 to 45 minutes, over medium-high heat, or until vegetables are tender.

- Add the cilantro leaves to the soup and cook for 5 minutes longer.

- Ladle the soup into individual soup bowls, cups or a large tureen. Sprinkle with scallions. Serve with warmed tortilla chips.

Antebellum Clam Chowder

Apparently, prior to the War Between the States, Southern-style clam chowder resembled the modern "New York Style" using a tomato base rather than milk. Clam chowder often appeared on Thanksgiving menus.

Serves 6

½ **pound fat pork (salt pork)**

2 to 3 medium-sized onions, coarsely chopped

4 to 6 large potatoes, peeled and cubed

1 quart clams with liquor

2 pounds canned tomatoes with juice

- Bring a saucepan of water to a boil. Plunge the pork into the water and simmer for 10 minutes. Remove pork from the water, drain, cool and cut into dice. (This blanching process helps to remove the excess salt from the salt pork.)

- In a large, heavy non-corrosive kettle (enamel or stainless steel), fry the pork over low heat to render the fat and crisp the meat. When the meat is crisp, remove from the pan. Sauté the onions in the pork fat until translucent.

- To the kettle, add the cubed potatoes, the clam liquor and enough hot water to cover. Simmer until the potatoes are tender. Then add the clams, crisp pork and tomatoes. Heat to warm through and serve in warm soup bowls or tureen.

"Old people shouldn't eat health foods. They need all the preservatives they can get."

Robert Orben

$\mathcal{S}$ *alads*

The Gazebo.
During the restoration years this gazebo, one of a pair which flank the mansion on its east terrace, was built, based on an early account of there having been "two bowers" at Kenmore in the time of Betty Lewis. The splendid tree pictured is a yellowwood (*cledastris lutea*), an American native. Kenmore's is the largest in Virginia!

Warm String Bean and New Potato Salad

Serves 6 to 8

2 pounds string beans

2 pounds small red potatoes

2 large onions, coarsely chopped

1 1-inch piece salt pork

Salt and freshly ground black pepper to taste

Dressing:

2 tablespoons freshly squeezed lemon juice

3 tablespoons safflower oil

2 tablespoons olive oil

1 teaspoon salt, or to taste

1 generous teaspoon powdered mustard

¼ teaspoon freshly ground black pepper

Chopped parsley for garnish

- Wash beans and snap into several pieces; remove ends. Scrub potatoes. If the potato size is irregular, you may halve or quarter some of them for consistent size.

- In a large saucepan, combine beans and potatoes; cover with water and add the onions and salt pork. Simmer 30 to 40 minutes. The beans should be very tender. Keep vegetables warm in their cooking water while making the dressing.

- Whisk together dressing ingredients. Drain the vegetables and toss with the dressing. Garnish with chopped parsley.

Wild Rice and Raisin Salad

Serves 4

½ **cup wild rice**

½ **cup pecan halves**

½ **pound lean ham**

¾ **cup golden raisins**

½ **cup thinly sliced green onions**

⅓ **cup olive oil**

¼ **cup rice wine vinegar**

¼ **teaspoon pepper**

- Wash rice. Cook in boiling water until tender. Rinse under hot running water; drain well.

- Spread pecan halves on a baking sheet and toast in a 350° oven for 10 minutes to enhance the flavor.

- Cut ham into julienne strips, about 1-inch long. Soak raisins in hot water and drain.

- Toss together wild rice, ham, raisins and green onions. Whisk together the olive oil, vinegar and pepper. Pour over rice; toss, cover, and chill.

- Serve salad on lettuce leaves, garnish with pecan halves.

Note: A delicious accompaniment to any roasted meats, especially a pork roast, in which case the ham may be optional.

Jicama, Orange and Avocado Salad

Jicama is a brown, bulbous root vegetable. The thin skin is easy to peel and the white inside is crunchy and moist with a mild, sweet flavor. It is popular in Mexican cooking.

Serves 4 to 6

1 large jicama (about 1½ pounds)

1 tablespoon finely chopped fresh cilantro

1 teaspoon salt

2 teaspoons finely grated grapefruit rind

2 tablespoons lemon juice

5 tablespoons orange juice

5 tablespoons grapefruit juice

1 large navel orange

1 ripe avocado

- Peel the jicama and dice into ½-inch cubes. Combine jicama with the fruit juices, salt, cilantro and rind. Set aside for at least one hour.

- Peel and slice the orange into thin slices. Halve and peel the avocado, cut into wedges.

- On a large platter, alternate orange and avocado slices. Spoon the jicama mixture over the top, sprinkling the fruit with some of the juice. Chill and serve.

Cotija Chicken Salad

Serves 6

1 3 to 4 pound whole chicken

1 rib celery, coarsely chopped

1 carrot, coarsely chopped

1 small onion, coarsely chopped

1 bay leaf

1 parsley sprig

2 tablespoons olive oil

Salt and pepper to taste

1 large red onion, thinly sliced

1 bunch radishes, sliced

2 bunches cilantro

¾ pound (about 3 cups) Cotija cheese (available in Mexican markets)

½ cup freshly squeezed lime juice

2 cups Fresh Mexican Salsa (recipe follows)

Fresh Mexican Salsa:

2 large ripe tomatoes

1 medium onion

10 sprigs cilantro

3 chilies, preferably serranos

½ teaspoon salt

½ cup cold water

- In large pot, place chicken and cover with cold water. Add the celery, carrot, onion, bay leaf, parsley sprig. Bring the water to a boil then reduce to a simmer. Simmer uncovered for 45 minutes to 1 hour, or until tender. Let the chicken cool in the broth for 2 hours. Remove chicken from broth and shred. Sprinkle with olive oil, salt and pepper. Toss to mix and refrigerate.

- Pick the leaves from the cilantro. Chop half of the cilantro, reserve the other for garnish. Crumble the Cotija cheese, reserve 1 cup of cheese for garnish.

- Combine the shredded chicken, onions, radishes, chopped cilantro, Fresh Salsa and Cotija cheese. Toss with lime juice and chill until serving time. Place on a lettuce lined platter or plate and garnish with cilantro leaves and 1 cup Cotija cheese.

• • •

- Chop the tomato, onion, cilantro and chilies finely. Combine in a bowl with salt and cold water.

Turkey, Orange and Belgian Endive Salad
with Tea and Szechuan Pepper Dressing

Serves 4

The Salad:

½ **cup boiling water**

1½ **teaspoons Lapsang Souchong tea**

12 **small slices smoked turkey, 4" x 2" (about ¾ pound)**

12 **mustard green leaves, washed, trimmed and dried**

3 **oranges, peeled and cut in ¼-inch slices**

16 **Belgian endive leaves**

The Dressing:

2 **tablespoons cider vinegar**

1 **teaspoon grated orange rind**

½ **small white onion**

Salt and freshly ground black pepper

6 **tablespoons corn oil**

1 **teaspoon finely powdered, untoasted Szechuan pepper**

- In a small bowl, pour the boiling water over the tea and let steep for 10 minutes, covered.

- Roll the slices of turkey into cornucopias and fill the hollow with the mustard greens. Arrange the turkey cornucopias alternately with orange slices and Belgian endive leaves on individual salad plates. Garnish with any leftover mustard greens.

• • •

- Mix the vinegar and orange rind. Grate the onion directly into the mixture. Add salt and pepper to taste. Strain 3 tablespoons of the tea into this mixture, add the corn oil, and whisk to blend thoroughly. Pour dressing over the salad and sprinkle with the powdered Szechuan pepper.

Note: This is an adaptation of a recipe from Madeleine Kamman.

Goat Cheese Fritters with Herbed Greens
on Basil Tomato Vinaigrette

Serves 2

The Fritters:
  1 8-ounce log goat cheese

  ½ cup flour

  2 egg whites, beaten frothy

  ½ cup ground saifan noodles (fine dry bread crumbs are an acceptable alternative)

The Basil Tomato Vinaigrette:
  3 tomatoes, peeled and seeded

  Juice of 2 lemons (about ½ cup)

  ¼ teaspoon fresh minced garlic

  1 tablespoon olive oil

  3 tablespoons chopped fresh basil

  Salt and freshly ground white pepper to taste

The Salad:
  2 cups arugula

  ½ cup sweet basil

  ½ cup opal basil

  1 small shallot, minced

  2 tablespoons olive oil

  Juice of 1 lemon

  Freshly ground black pepper to taste

- Cut cheese log into ½-inch thick medallions. Dust with flour, dip in egg whites and into the saifan noodles (or breadcrumbs). Fry the fritters in 350° vegetable oil just until crisp. Set aside.

   •   •   •

- In a blender jar, combine 1 tomato with lemon juice, garlic, olive oil and basil; purée. Add remaining tomatoes and pulse to chop coarsely. Set aside.

   •   •   •

- Wash greens, remove stems, and dry. Combine shallot, olive oil, lemon juice and pepper; toss with greens.

To Serve:
- Divide greens between two plates, covering ⅔ of the plates. Spoon the Basil Tomato Vinaigrette on the other ⅓ of the plate. Place the Goat Cheese Fritters overlapping each other on top of the vinaigrette. Garnish with a sprig of opal basil.

Note: This recipe was developed by Chef John Makin for Duckworth Restaurant, St. Helena, California.

Salad of Pears and Stilton with Sage Leaves

Serves 4

1 teaspoon Dijon-style mustard

1½ tablespoons champagne vinegar

⅓ cup light olive oil

¼ teaspoon salt

¼ teaspoon freshly ground black pepper

4 tablespoons unsalted butter

24 large fresh sage leaves (whole leaves)

2 tablespoons chopped sage leaves

2 cups French bread cubes, ½-inch cubes

2 ripe pears, preferably Bosc

½ head Boston lettuce (butter, or bibb lettuce)

½ head escarole

½ head romaine

½ head red leaf lettuce

½ cup thinly sliced red onion

3 ounces Stilton cheese, crumbled

¼ cup sage blossoms (optional)

- In a small bowl, whisk together the mustard, vinegar, olive oil, salt and pepper. Set the vinaigrette aside.

- In a large skillet, melt 1 tablespoon of the butter over moderate heat. Add the sage leaves. Increase the heat to moderately high and dry until the leaves are golden brown and crisp on the bottom, about 1 minute. Turn the leaves and cook until crisp on the second side, about 1 minute longer. Remove to a plate.

- Melt the remaining 3 tablespoons butter in the same skillet over moderate heat. Add the bread cubes and sprinkle the chopped sage over them. Toss to coat the bread evenly with the butter and sage. Cook, turning occasionally, until the cubes are golden brown and crunchy, about 4 minutes. Season the croutons with an additional pinch of salt.

- Peel, core, and halve the pears. Slice into ¼-inch thick wedges. In a medium bowl, toss the pears with 2 tablespoons of the vinaigrette until evenly coated.

- Tear the lettuces into bite-size pieces. Combine in large bowl with the red onion and toss with the remaining vinaigrette.

- Place an equal amount of lettuce on each of 4 large plates and arrange the pear slices on top. Sprinkle each salad with Stilton cheese and top with the toasted sage leaves, croutons and sage blossoms, if available.

Orange and Fennel Salad

Serves 4

1½ pounds fennel bulbs, cut into thin slivers

2 tablespoons chopped fennel leaves

4 navel oranges

1 tablespoon balsamic vinegar

¼ teaspoon salt

2 tablespoons extra-virgin olive oil

- In a large salad bowl or on individual plates, arrange a bed of slivered fennel.

- Peel and slice the oranges into ¼-inch thick slices. Overlap orange slices on top of the fennel.

- In a small bowl, whisk the vinegar and salt together. Gradually whisk in the oil. Drizzle the dressing over the oranges and fennel; garnish with the fennel leaves.

Baked Beet and Endive Salad

Serves 6

2 bunches of beets, with ½-inch tops

2 teaspoons green peppercorn mustard

¼ cup balsamic vinegar

2 teaspoons salt

1 teaspoon freshly ground black pepper

¼ cup plus 2 tablespoons safflower oil

¼ cup light olive oil

4 heads Belgian endive, separated into individual leaves

2 tablespoons chopped chives

- Preheat oven to 425°. Line a roasting pan with foil. Place the beets in the pan in a single layer. Cover the pan with foil and bake until the beets are tender, about 1 hour.

- When the beets are done, let them cool slightly. Remove the tops and slip off the skins. Cut the beets into ½-inch wedges.

- In a small bowl, combine the mustard, vinegar, salt and pepper. Slowly whisk in the safflower oil and olive oil.

- In a medium bowl, toss the beets with three-quarters of the vinaigrette. Arrange the endive leaves on a large plate, pour the remaining dressing on top and sprinkle with chopped chives.

Vegetable Antipasto

Serves 6

10 ounces green beans

4 carrots

3 celery ribs

½ small head cauliflower

4 cups water

1 teaspoon salt

¼ pound mushrooms

3 tablespoons chopped parsley

Vinaigrette Dressing:
2 tablespoons red wine vinegar

8 tablespoons olive oil

1 teaspoon Dijon-style mustard

1 teaspoon lemon juice

1 teaspoon salt

Freshly ground pepper to taste

- Wash the beans, trim ends, and cut in half on the bias.

- Scrape the carrots and slice thinly on the bias. Put the carrots into a bowl of cold water.

- Wash the celery and shave off any tough fibers with a vegetable peeler. Slice on the bias.

- Break up the cauliflower into bite-sized pieces and add to the cold water with the carrots.

- Bring the water and salt to a boil. Add the carrots and celery and cook for 4 minutes. Remove with a slotted spoon and set aside. Add the cauliflower to the same water and cook at a rolling boil for 4 minutes. Remove with a slotted spoon and set aside. Add the green beans to the water, bring to a boil, and drain immediately.

- Wipe the mushrooms with a clean damp cloth and slice them very thin.

- In a bowl, combine all the drained vegetables with the mushrooms and parsley. Toss well with the Vinaigrette Dressing. Serve on lettuce leaves.

• • •

- Combine all ingredients and whisk until well blended.

Sweet and Sour Broccoli Salad

Serves 8 to 10

3 bunches broccoli, tops only

1 pound bacon, cooked and crumbled

½ red onion, chopped

1 cup raisins

¾ cup sunflower seeds

Dressing:

1 cup mayonnaise

¼ cup sugar

2 tablespoons rice wine vinegar

- Cut broccoli into florets. Plunge into boiling salted water to partially cook. Cook a few at a time and refresh the broccoli in a bowl of iced water. Remove from iced water and drain thoroughly.

• • •

- Toss broccoli with raisins, bacon, onion. Combine mayonnaise, sugar and vinegar and toss again. Chill overnight.

- At serving time, add sunflower seeds, toss and serve.

Twenty-four Hour Vegetable Salad

Serves 12

1 small head iceberg lettuce, shredded

1 cup chopped celery

1 cup chopped scallions, using green tops

2 8½-ounce cans sliced water chestnuts

2 10-ounce packages frozen peas, thawed

1 cup chopped green pepper

Alfalfa sprouts

1 cup mayonnaise

1 cup sour cream

2 tablespoons granulated sugar

Parmesan cheese, freshly grated

Crumbled cooked bacon

- Layer lettuce, celery, scallions, water chestnuts, peas, green pepper and alfalfa sprouts in a glass bowl. Amounts may be varied.

- Combine mayonnaise, sour cream and sugar. Spread over the salad. Sprinkle generously with Parmesan cheese.

- Cover. Refrigerate for 24 hours.

- Before serving, garnish with chopped bacon. Do not toss!

Note: A colorful and tasty buffet salad.

Rogue River Mustard Ring with Coleslaw

Serves 8 to 10

Mustard Ring:
  ½ cup sugar

  1½ tablespoons dry mustard

  Dash of salt

  ¼ cup water

  1 envelope unflavored gelatin

  ¾ cup cider vinegar

  4 eggs, beaten

  1 cup heavy cream

Cole Slaw:
  1 small head cabbage, chopped

Dressing:
  1 cucumber, peeled and finely grated

  1 small onion, finely grated

  1 cup parsley, chopped

  1 cup sour cream

  ¼ cup mayonnaise

  1 teaspoon celery seed

  1 teaspoon dry mustard

  ½ teaspoon dill weed

  1 teaspoon wine vinegar

  ¼ cup sugar

  Juice of ½ lemon

  Salt and pepper to taste

- Combine sugar, mustard and salt. Soak gelatin in ¼ cup water and dissolve over hot water. Mix the dissolved gelatin with the vinegar and stir into the eggs, then add the dry ingredients. Cook in the top of a double boiler over simmering water, stirring constantly until thickened and creamy. Set aside to cool, but do not gel.

- Whip the heavy cream to soft peaks and fold gently into the mustard mixture. Oil a 3-cup ring mold and fill with the mustard-cream mixture. Chill until serving time. Unmold and fill center of ring with coleslaw.

•   •   •

- Combine all dressing ingredients and mix thoroughly with the chopped cabbage. Let stand at least 1 hour for flavors to blend.

Red Slaw Crook's Corner Style

Serves 8 to 12

1 16-ounce can Italian tomatoes, with juices

1 3-ounce jar pimientos, drained

2 pounds cabbage (1 small), finely chopped

1 small green bell pepper, chopped

½ cup apple cider vinegar

¼ cup sugar

¾ teaspoon salt

½ tablespoon hot pepper sauce, or to taste

⅛ teaspoon freshly ground black pepper

Pinch celery seed

- In a blender or food processor, purée tomatoes with the pimientos. Combine with the cabbage in a glass or pottery bowl.

- Add the remaining ingredients to the cabbage-to-mato mixture. Stir well, refrigerate for at least 2 hours and toss again before serving.

(Crook's Corner is a restaurant in Chapel Hill, North Carolina owned and operated by Bill Neal.)

Sicilian Green Bean and Fennel Salad

Serves 8

½ pound fresh green beans

1⅔ cups thinly sliced fennel bulb (1 large)

½ cup julienned red bell pepper

2 tablespoons lemon juice

1 tablespoon olive oil

½ teaspoon grated orange rind

⅛ teaspoon salt

⅛ teaspoon freshly ground black pepper

1 clove garlic, minced

1 tablespoon minced fennel leaves

- Wash green beans, trim ends and remove strings. Cut the beans in half. Arrange in a vegetable steamer and place over boiling water. Cover and steam 5 minutes or until crisp-tender. Drain beans and plunge into a bowl of ice water, drain again.

- Combine beans, sliced fennel and bell pepper in a bowl. Toss gently and set aside.

- Combine next six ingredients, mix well. Pour this dressing over the vegetables and toss gently to coat. Sprinkle with the fennel leaves. Serve chilled or at room temperature.

Delta Point Salad

Serves 10 to 12

Marinated vegetables:
  ½ **pound small button mushrooms**

  2 **cups hearts of palm, cut into chunks**

  2 **cups artichoke hearts, quartered**

Marinade:
  ½ **cup vegetable oil**

  ½ **cup virgin olive oil**

  ½ **cup red wine vinegar**

  2 **teaspoons minced fresh oregano (1 teaspoon dried)**

  2 **teaspoons minced fresh basil (1 teaspoon dried)**

  Salt and freshly ground black pepper to taste

The Salad:
  2 **cups iceberg lettuce**

  2 **cups romaine lettuce**

  2 **cups curly leaf lettuce**

  1 **cup red radishes, sliced**

  1 **cup carrots, sliced**

  1 **cup cauliflower florets**

  1 **basket cherry tomatoes**

- Combine mushrooms, hearts of palm and artichoke hearts. If mushrooms are large, halve or quarter them to be of compatible size with the other vegetables.

•   •   •

- Combine oils, vinegar, herbs, salt and pepper. Toss dressing over vegetables and marinate for at least 4 hours.

•   •   •

- Tear the lettuces into bite-size pieces. Combine with radishes, carrots, cauliflower and cherry tomatoes. Remove marinated vegetables from their marinade (reserve marinade for future use), and add to lettuce mixture.

•   •   •

Continued on next page

The Dressing:

1 cup mayonnaise

1 cup buttermilk

¼ teaspoon minced garlic

2 teaspoons minced onion

½ teaspoon Beau Monde Seasoning

2 teaspoons chopped parsley

2 teaspoons chopped chives

¼ teaspoon celery salt

⅛ teaspoon freshly ground black pepper

- Combine all ingredients and mix well. Refrigerate overnight. Makes 2 cups.

Note: This dressing is a fresh, homemade alternative to "ranch style" dressings.

Wilted Lettuce

Serves 4 to 6

Fresh garden lettuce (Boston/Bibb or leafy red or green)

4 scallions, thinly sliced

5 or 6 slices bacon

2 slices country ham

½ cup cider vinegar

3 teaspoons sugar

¼ cup water

1 teaspoon salt

½ teaspoon freshly ground black pepper

- Wash, dry and tear the lettuce into bite size pieces. Refrigerate until ready to use. Sprinkle with scallions.

- In a medium skillet, sauté the bacon with the two slices of ham. Remove the meat from the skillet, drain on paper towels, crumble the bacon and dice the ham. Set aside.

- To the fat in the skillet, add the vinegar, sugar, water, salt and pepper. Bring to a boil and pour over the lettuce-scallion mixture.

- Garnish with the crumbled bacon and diced ham. Serve at once.

Hoppin' John Vinaigrette

Serves 10 to 12

2 cups dried black-eyed peas and water to cover

2 quarts water

½ pound country ham (or 1 meat ham bone)

1 cup rice, uncooked

1 cup chopped onion

1 cup chopped celery

1 bay leaf

1 teaspoon chopped fresh oregano

1 teaspoon chopped fresh rosemary

1 teaspoon sugar

2 teaspoons salt

½ teaspoon freshly ground black pepper

Vinaigrette:

1 medium onion, chopped

⅓ cup red wine vinegar

1 tablespoon Dijon-style mustard

1 cup peanut oil

Salt to taste

Freshly ground black pepper to taste

2 tablespoons chopped fresh basil

3 to 4 heads seasonal lettuce greens

4 strips bacon, fried crisp and crumbled

- Sort and wash black-eyed peas. Place in a heavy saucepan and add water to cover. Cover the saucepan and bring to a boil. Immediately remove from the heat. With lid in place, soak peas 1 hour and drain.

- Combine ham and 2 quarts water in a large Dutch oven. Bring to a boil. Reduce heat, cover and simmer 45 minutes.

- Add the bay leaf, oregano, rosemary, sugar, salt and pepper. Bring to a boil. Reduce heat, cover and simmer an additional 30 minutes, or until the black-eyed peas are done. Remove ham and dice. Stir ham back into the bean mixture.

• • •

- The vinaigrette: Add the chopped onion to the Hoppin' John mixture and toss to combine. In a small bowl, mix the vinegar and mustard then slowly whisk in the oil. Season to taste with salt and pepper. Add dressing to Hoppin' John along with the basil. Toss to combine. Serve hot or cold.

- To serve cold: Arrange lettuce leaves on serving plates. Spoon Hoppin' John Vinaigrette onto center of the leaves. Garnish with crumbled bacon.

Note: This is an adaptation of a recipe from Southern Cooking by Natalie Dupree.

Rosemary Dressing

Makes 2 cups

1½ cups raspberry vinegar

¼ cup chopped rosemary

⅛ cup chopped lemon basil

1 tablespoon honey

¼ cup raspberries

¼ cup sesame oil

¼ cup water

⅛ teaspoon nutmeg

- Combine all ingredients in a blender and blend for 1 minute. Store in the refrigerator.

Ginger Soy Dressing

Makes 2½ cups

1½ cups rice vinegar

¼ cup light soy sauce

½ cup water

1½ tablespoons minced fresh ginger

2 tablespoons minced shallot

½ teaspoon five spice mixture (available in Asian markets)

¼ cup minced scallions

1 tablespoon honey

1 tablespoon dark sesame oil

2 tablespoons light sesame oil

- Combine all ingredients and mix thoroughly. Store in the refrigerator.

Note: This is a good dressing for any Asian-style salad, spinach salad or chicken salad.

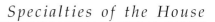

Mah Pe Salad Dressing

This was the house dressing for Edith Palmer's Country Inn, Virginia City, Nevada.

Makes 2 cups

2 teaspoons salt

1 teaspoon freshly ground black pepper

2 teaspoons dry mustard

3 teaspoons Worcestershire sauce

2 tablespoons red wine vinegar

6 tablespoons malt vinegar

1 cup olive oil

2 cloves garlic, split

- Combine all ingredients in a jar. Shake well and allow to stand to blend flavors. Serve with crisp, sharp greens.

Basic Vinaigrette

Serves 2 to 4

1 tablespoon wine vinegar

½ teaspoon salt

Freshly ground black pepper

½ teaspoon Dijon-style mustard

3 tablespoons olive oil

- Whisk vinegar, salt, pepper and mustard together until blended.

- Whisk in oil and pour over greens.

Note: Substitute different flavors of vinegar, mustard and oils to complement various salad greens.

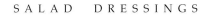

A More Subtle Vinaigrette

Serves 4 to 6

2 tablespoons white wine vinegar

½ teaspoon salt

Freshly ground black pepper

½ teaspoon Dijon-style mustard

½ teaspoon Moutarde de Meaux (grainy)

6 tablespoons olive oil

- Whisk vinegar, salt, pepper and mustard together until well blended.

- Whisk in oil and pour over greens.

Creamy Vinaigrette

Makes 1 cup

5 tablespoons tarragon vinegar

2 teaspoons salt

1 teaspoon freshly ground black pepper

½ teaspoon Dijon-style mustard

1 garlic clove, minced

⅔ cup olive oil

1 small egg, lightly beaten

½ cup half-and-half

Chopped parsley for garnish

- Thoroughly mix all ingredients to blend.

Note: This is a creamy alternative to a basic vinaigrette. It is excellent for a cold vegetable platter-salad. Dress blanched vegetables at the last minute so they will not discolor from the vinegar's acid.

"We may live without poetry, music and art;
We may live without conscience, and live without heart;
We may live without friends; we may live without books;
But civilized man cannot live without cooks."

Owen Meredith

$\mathcal{V}$egetables

Appraisers found Fielding Lewis' dining room closet
filled with "Sundry Chinia, Glassware" and "Plate"
when they inventoried his estate in 1782.

Those Potatoes

Serves 6

5 tablespoons butter

5 tablespoons flour

2 cups half-and-half (light cream), scalded

⅔ cup homemade chicken stock

5 tablespoons freshly grated Parmesan cheese

1 teaspoon salt

½ teaspoon freshly ground white pepper

2 pounds potatoes, cooked, peeled and diced

¾ cup crumbled Roquefort cheese

¼ cup butter, melted

Paprika

- Melt butter in a saucepan. Add flour and whisk over low heat for 2 minutes. Remove pan from heat. Gradually stir in the cream and the stock. Return pan to heat. Cook and stir sauce until it is smooth and thickened. Stir in the Parmesan cheese, salt and pepper.

- Gently fold the potatoes into the cheese sauce. Taste for seasoning; add more salt and pepper if needed.

- Divide the potato mixture between 6 individual buttered ramekins (or a 2-quart au gratin dish). Sprinkle with Roquefort cheese, melted butter and paprika.

- Bake in a 425° oven for 12 to 14 minutes for individual servings, 20 to 25 minutes for large dish, or until cheese bubbles.

Stuffed Baked Potato with Broccoli and Cheese

Serves 4

4 large baking potatoes

½ cup low fat plain yogurt

½ cup low fat cottage cheese

2 tablespoons whole grain mustard

2 ribs of celery, chopped

2 tablespoons chopped chives

½ teaspoon freshly ground black pepper

1 cup steamed broccoli flowerettes

4 slices low fat Mozzarella cheese

- Place the potatoes on a baking sheet and bake at 350° for 1 hour or until done. Let cool slightly.

- Cut a circle off the tops of the potatoes. Scoop out the pulp and put in a mixing bowl. Add the yogurt, mustard, cottage cheese, celery, chives and pepper. Mix well with a potato masher.

- Spoon the potato mixture back into the potato shell, mounding the tops with the steamed broccoli flowerettes and 1 slice Mozzarella cheese on top of each. Bake at 350° for 10 to 15 minutes or until hot and cheese has melted.

Sweet Potato Pudding

Serves 6 to 8

2 large sweet potatoes

Milk to cover

4 eggs

1 cup sugar

½ cup butter, melted

1 small can condensed milk

Pinch of salt

1 teaspoon vanilla

- Preheat oven to 350°.

- Generously butter a 9" x 13" baking dish.

- Peel the sweet potatoes. Chop coarsely and put into a blender, cover with milk. Chop briefly in the blender until they reach the consistency of coarsely grated coconut.

- To the blender add the eggs, sugar, butter, condensed milk, salt and vanilla. Blend just to mix.

- Pour the potato mixture into the prepared baking dish. Put in the preheated oven and bake 30 to 45 minutes, or until firm and brown. Serve warm.

Waterless Baked Asparagus

Serves 4

1 pound asparagus tips, about 4½-inches long

Salt and freshly ground pepper

3 tablespoons butter, cut in small pieces

- In a shallow baking dish, layer asparagus closely together in no more than 2 layers. Sprinkle with salt and pepper; dot with butter. Cover dish tightly with foil.

- Bake at 300° for 25 minutes.

Note: Pencil-thin asparagus may require less cooking time.

Asparagus with Sesame-Ginger Sauce

Serves 4

1 pound fresh asparagus

1½ teaspoons sesame seeds

¼ cup freshly squeezed orange juice

1 tablespoon soy sauce

½ teaspoon cornstarch

½ teaspoon sugar

¼ teaspoon peeled, grated ginger root

¼ cup water

- Wash asparagus and trim off the tough stem end.

- In a small nonstick skillet, toast the sesame seeds just until golden brown. About 1 minute. Watch carefully so they don't burn. Remove from heat and set aside.

- Combine orange juice, soy sauce, cornstarch, sugar and grated ginger. In a medium-sized skillet with a cover, place the asparagus with ¼ cup water. Place over high heat, cover and cook for 5 to 7 minutes. Uncover, stir the juice mixture again, and add to the asparagus, tossing to coat. Cook for another 3 to 5 minutes (depending on size of asparagus) until the asparagus is just tender and the sauce is thickened. Sprinkle with the toasted sesame seeds.

Pernod Spinach

Serves 4

1 pound spinach

2 teaspoons Pernod

1 tablespoon butter, melted

Salt and freshly ground black pepper

⅛ teaspoon freshly grated nutmeg

- Wash spinach and with water still clinging to the leaves, cook in a covered saucepan just until wilted. Drain in a sieve, blotting with paper towels to dry thoroughly.

- Put spinach and other ingredients in a food processor; purée. Adjust seasonings to taste. Serve warm.

Spinach with Lemon and Toasted Sesame Seeds

Serves 4

2 pounds fresh spinach, washed and stemmed

1 tablespoon sesame seeds

1 tablespoon Japanese soy sauce

1½ teaspoons fresh lemon juice

1½ teaspoons granulated sugar

- In a large covered saucepan, steam the spinach, in the water clinging to the leaves, over moderately high heat for 3 minutes. Rinse under cold water, drain, and squeeze out excess moisture.

- In a small skillet, toast the sesame seeds over moderately high heat, shaking the pan until the first seeds pop, 1 to 2 minutes. Set aside.

- In a large bowl, combine the soy sauce, lemon juice and sugar; stir until the sugar is dissolved. Add the spinach and toss well.

- Divide the spinach among four small bowls and sprinkle a quarter of the toasted sesame seeds over each. Serve at room temperature or chilled.

Spinach Ravioli/Ravioli Nudi

Serves 6

2 packages frozen spinach

1 pound ricotta cheese

1 egg

2 egg yolks

⅛ teaspoon freshly grated nutmeg

Salt and freshly ground black pepper

1 clove garlic, finely minced

½ cup freshly grated Parmesan cheese

4 tablespoons unsalted butter, melted

½ cup freshly grated Parmesan cheese

- Cook spinach according to instructions. Do not overcook. Cool and squeeze dry and chop fine.

- Drain ricotta cheese well and combine with spinach, egg, egg yolks, nutmeg, salt, pepper, garlic and ½ cup Parmesan cheese. Blend well and refrigerate to chill.

- On a floured surface and with flour-dusted hands, roll spinach mixture into a long log 1-inch in diameter. Cut in 2-inch pieces and lightly flour each end. Recipe may be made ahead to this point.

- Fill a large stock pot or pasta pot with water. Bring to a boil. Plunge the ravioli, a few at a time, into the boiling water. The ravioli will rise to the top when done. Remove from the water with a slotted spoon.

- To serve, stack ravioli like a stack of cordwood on a platter. Drizzle with melted butter and sprinkle with Parmesan cheese.

Note: The "nudi" part of the name refers to the fact that the filling is not covered with pasta.

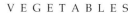

Artichoke Delight

Serves 4

4 large artichokes

½ pound mushroom caps

Juice of 2 lemons

2 tablespoons butter

1½ cups heavy cream

½ cup freshly grated Parmesan cheese

- Cook artichokes in simmering water for 45 minutes. Discard leaves and chokes. Place artichoke bottoms in a flat baking dish.

- Wipe the mushroom caps with a paper towel saturated with lemon juice. In a medium skillet melt the butter and sauté the mushroom caps with the remaining lemon juice, cooking slowly until the juices are reduced.

- Add cream to the mushrooms to cover. Continue cooking over low heat until much of the cream is absorbed, reserving some to pour over the artichokes later. Remove from heat.

- Fill artichoke bottoms with mushrooms and cream sauce. Sprinkle with Parmesan cheese; place under broiler to warm through and brown lightly.

Note: A rich yet flavorful first course purportedly from Jacqueline Kennedy during her White House years. This may be prepared in advance and placed in a 350° oven for 20 minutes to reheat.

Parsleyed Cucumbers

Serves 6

6 cucumbers

6 tablespoons butter

Salt

Freshly ground white pepper

8 to 10 parsley sprigs, minced

- Peel the cucumbers, then cut each one into four pieces and cut each of those pieces into four again. Trim the individual pieces into neat ovals the size of a large garlic clove.

- In a large saucepan, bring water to a boil, drop the cucumbers into the water and cook until just tender when pierced with a sharp knife, 8 to 10 minutes. With a slotted spoon, lift the cucumbers from the boiling water, refresh in cold water (to stop the cooking), drain, and set aside. Cover with a damp towel.

- Melt the butter in a heavy skillet. When it foams, add half the cucumbers, salt and pepper and sauté quickly. Drain on paper towels. Arrange in a heated vegetable dish and keep warm. Sauté the remaining cucumbers. Combine the two and mix in the minced parsley.

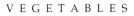

Pasta Alla Puttanesca
(Pasta with a Sauce of Uncooked Tomatoes and Herbs)

Serves 4

1 pound very ripe tomatoes or 12-ounces canned tomatoes

4 cloves of garlic, chopped

25 large leaves fresh basil

½ cup olive oil

Salt

Freshly ground black pepper

1 pound dried pasta, shells, snails or penne

- Cut tomatoes into small pieces and put in a bowl with the garlic. Tear basil leaves into thirds and add to the bowl, along with the oil, salt and pepper. Toss ingredients together, cover tightly and place in the refrigerator for at least 2 hours before serving.

- Put a large pot of salted water on the heat. When the water boils, cook the pasta until al dente (about 12 minutes). Drain quickly and place in a serving bowl.

- While pasta is extremely hot, pour the refrigerated sauce over it. Toss well and serve at once. (Do not serve with grated cheese.)

Cabbage Pie

Serves 6 to 8

7 cups shredded cabbage

3 cups saltine crackers, coarsely crumbled

2 cups milk

¼ cup butter

½ teaspoon freshly ground black pepper

½ teaspoon celery seed

- Preheat oven to 350°.

- Butter a 1½-quart casserole. Alternate layers of cabbage and coarsely crumbled crackers; begin with cabbage and end with crackers.

- In a medium saucepan, heat milk and add butter, pepper and celery seed; pour over the cabbage-cracker mixture.

- Bake in the preheated oven for 40 minutes or until lightly browned on the top.

Note: If using unsalted crackers, 1 teaspoon salt may be added.

Roast Garlic and Sage Polenta

Serves 6

1 large head garlic, separated into cloves, unpeeled

4 tablespoons olive oil

12 large mushrooms, stems and caps separated

1 tablespoon butter

2¼ cups chicken stock

2½ cups coarse cornmeal

½ cup small corn kernels, cooked

5 tablespoons sweet butter, cut in small pieces

1 tablespoon chopped fresh sage

Salt

Pepper

Parmesan cheese, freshly grated (to taste, about ½ cup)

1¼ pounds sweet butter, clarified*

- Toss garlic cloves in oil. Roast on baking sheet in a 350° oven for 30 minutes. Let cool; peel, and mash garlic into a pulp. Set aside.

- Mince the mushroom stems, and sauté in 1 tablespoon butter.

- In a heavy pot, bring chicken stock and mushroom stems to a boil. Add 2 cups of cornmeal in a steady stream, stirring with a wooden spoon. Lower heat, and cook for 10 minutes, stirring frequently. Add corn, butter pieces, sage, garlic, salt, pepper and Parmesan cheese.

- Spread 3 layers of plastic wrap (about 13-inches long) on the counter. Spread the polenta mixture in an 11-inch log. Wrap and mold into a sausage shape 3-inches in diameter. Chill until firm, at least 4 hours.

- Slice mushroom caps in very thin rounds. In a deep saucepan, heat the clarified butter, and slowly deep fry the mushroom slices over medium heat until crisp. Drain on paper towels and season with salt. Set aside.

- Cut polenta into 12 slices. Dredge in the remaining ½ cup cornmeal, and sauté a few at a time in some of the clarified butter until golden brown; drain on paper towels. Garnish with mushroom chips.

*To clarify butter: Put the butter in a large glass measuring cup in a warm oven (or microwave) and let it stand until it melts and the milky substance settles at the bottom. You can strain the clear liquid at the top into a container through damp cheesecloth or just put the melted butter in the refrigerator to harden and scrape off the milky residue.

Hominy Balls

Serves 4

1½ cups hominy

6 cups boiling water

3 cups milk

6 tablespoons butter

Salt

Nutmeg

2 eggs

2 egg yolks

1 egg, beaten

1 cup fine, dry breadcrumbs

2 tablespoons currant jelly (or other red jelly)

- Cook hominy in salted water in double boiler 1 hour or longer. Add hot milk and butter. Season to taste with salt and nutmeg. Beat eggs and egg yolks slightly and add to hot mixture. Cook 1 minute longer. Cool slightly before shaping.

- Shape hominy mixture into patties about 3-inches in diameter and 1¼-inches thick. Roll in breadcrumbs; then in beaten egg and again in the crumbs. Fry in deep fat until golden brown. Make a depression in one side with a teaspoon for spot of bright jelly.

Grits and Green Chilies

Serves 8

1½ cups hominy grits

6 cups water

¾ cup butter

1 pound sharp Cheddar cheese, grated

1 teaspoon salt

1 teaspoon Tabasco

3 eggs, beaten

2 small cans Ortega green chilies

- Butter a 9" x 13" oven-proof casserole.

- In a large saucepan, combine the grits and water, bring to a boil and cook for 5 minutes.

- Add the butter, cheese, salt, Tabasco, eggs and chilies (with seeds and juices) to the grits.

- Pour into the prepared casserole and refrigerate 12 to 24 hours before baking.

- Bake in a preheated 350° oven for 1 hour or until nicely browned.

111

Grits Soufflé

Serves 8

4½ cups water

½ teaspoon salt

2 teaspoons sugar

1 cup quick-cooking hominy grits

¼ pound butter, cut into pieces

4 eggs, slightly beaten

¼ teaspoon garlic powder

Dash Tabasco sauce

2 cups grated sharp Cheddar cheese

½ cup dry breadcrumbs

½ teaspoon paprika

- Preheat oven to 350°.

- In a heavy 4-quart saucepan, bring water to boiling and add the salt, sugar and grits. Cook 3 to 5 minutes, stirring constantly.

- Remove saucepan from the heat and add the butter, eggs, garlic powder, Tabasco and cheese. Stir well to blend thoroughly.

- Butter the bottom and sides of a 2½-quart soufflé dish or other straight-sided baking dish. Sprinkle with 2 tablespoons of the breadcrumbs to coat.

- Pour the prepared grits mixture into the prepared baking dish. Sprinkle with breadcrumbs and paprika. Bake in the preheated oven for 1 hour. Serve at once.

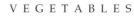

Angel's Quick Grits Soufflé, Lyford Cay

Serves 4

¾ **cup instant grits (3 packages)**

¾ **cup milk**

¾ **cup water**

½ **teaspoon salt (or less)**

½ **cup sweet butter**

6 ounces sharp Cheddar cheese, grated

3 eggs, lightly beaten

- Preheat oven to 350°.

- In the top of a double boiler, or a heavy-bottomed saucepan, place the grits, milk, water and salt. Cook stirring constantly until the mixture starts to boil.

- In a 1-quart soufflé dish, place the butter and grated cheese. Add the cooked grits, blending until the cheese and butter are melted. Cool slightly, then beat in the eggs.

- Bake on the middle rack of the preheated oven for 35 to 40 minutes, or until the soufflé has puffed and the top is slightly browned.

Note: When doubling the recipe, use a 2-quart soufflé dish and bake for 1 hour and 10 minutes.

This soufflé is a great side dish for roast chicken.

Red Onion Tart

Serves 6

1 pre-baked 9-inch tart shell

8 onions, thinly sliced

6 tablespoons butter

¼ cup granulated sugar

½ cup red wine vinegar

¼ cup Cassis

¾ cup red wine

Salt and freshly ground black pepper

¼ cup freshly grated Parmesan cheese

¼ cup chopped parsley

- Preheat oven to 400°.

- In a large skillet, sauté onions in butter until translucent. Add sugar, red wine vinegar, Cassis and red wine; cook for 10 minutes, stirring frequently. Cover the skillet and cook for 5 minutes. Season with salt and pepper. Uncover and cook to evaporate the excess liquid.

- Pour onion mixture into the prepared tart shell. Sprinkle with Parmesan cheese.

- Bake in preheated oven for 5 minutes. Place under the broiler for 1 minute. Garnish with chopped parsley.

Note: The "red" onion comes from the red wine vinegar, the Cassis and the red wine, not from red or purple onions.

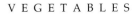

Shallot Purée

Serves 6

¾ **pound peeled shallots**

¼ **cup white wine vinegar**

½ **cup unsalted butter**

2 tablespoons chopped fresh thyme leaves (1 tablespoon dried)

1 bay leaf

1 teaspoon black peppercorns

1 cup heavy cream

1 garlic clove

Salt and freshly ground white pepper

- In a heavy saucepan, combine shallots, vinegar, butter, thyme, bay leaf and peppercorns. Cook slowly over low heat for 45 minutes or until shallots are soft.

- In another saucepan, heat cream and simmer to reduce it by half. Combine with the shallots; remove bay leaf.

- Press the mixture through a wide-mesh sieve or food mill with medium blade. Salt and pepper to taste and serve hot.

Note: This is a tasty accompaniment to roasted or grilled meats.

Justine's Celery Root and Pear Purée

From Justine's in Midland, Michigan, this is a delightful accompaniment to
pork roast or braised meats.

Serves 8

2 lemons

2 pounds celery root (celeriac)

½ teaspoon granulated sugar

2 ripe pears

12 tablespoons unsalted butter, softened

½ cup shallots

3 to 5 tablespoons heavy cream

½ teaspoon salt

¼ teaspoon freshly ground white pepper

Pinch of freshly grated nutmeg

- Fill a medium bowl with cold water. Add the juice from the lemons. Peel the celery root and cut into ½-inch dice. Immediately place in the acidulated water to prevent discoloration.

- Bring a large pot of salted water to a boil and add the sugar. With a slotted spoon, remove the celery root from the acidulated water and add to the boiling water (reserve the acidulated water). Cover partially and cook over moderately high heat until tender but not mushy, 5 to 8 minutes. Drain and set aside.

- Peel and core the pears. Cut into ½-inch dice and hold in the reserved acidulated water until ready to use.

- In a medium skillet, melt 2 tablespoons of the butter over low heat. Add the shallots and cook, covered, until translucent, about 5 minutes.

- Place the celery root in a food processor or blender and purée briefly. Drain the pears and add to the celery root. Scrape in the shallots with their butter and purée until smooth.

- In a small heavy saucepan, cook 6 tablespoons of the butter over moderate heat until golden brown and faintly nut scented, about 3 minutes. (Be careful not to burn the butter.) Immediately add to the purée and blend well. Press the purée through a fine-mesh sieve for a finer texture.

Continued on next page

- In a large heavy saucepan, combine the purée and 3 tablespoons of the cream. Cook, stirring, over low heat, until warm. Season with the salt, pepper and nutmeg. Stir in the remaining 4 tablespoons of butter, 1 tablespoon at a time. If not serving immediately hold in the top of a double boiler for up to 1 hour. Add the additional 2 tablespoons heavy cream as needed if the purée thickens too much.

Alice Waters' Long-Cooked Broccoli
with Anchovies and Parmesan on Croutons

Serves 6

2 pounds large broccoli (leaves and stems)

1 cup extra virgin olive oil

1 large head of garlic (about 2 ounces)

1½ teaspoons dried red pepper flakes

¾ cup water

1 teaspoon salt

½ teaspoon freshly ground black pepper

½ cup freshly squeezed lemon juice

1 tin anchovies packed in salt

Parmesan cheese, freshly grated

- Cut broccoli into small pieces including the stems and leaves, if any.

- Break the garlic head into cloves, peel and slice. Warm the olive oil in a heavy-bottomed casserole. Add the garlic, lemon juice, water, red pepper flakes, salt and pepper.

- Add the broccoli to the pan, simmer covered for approximately 45 minutes or until it is very tender. Stir the pot occasionally to prevent the broccoli from sticking.

- Serve the broccoli by itself, or arrange on toasted slices of French bread garnished with anchovies and Parmesan cheese.

Note: This broccoli is an excellent accompaniment to braised fish or grilled beef steak.

Mexican Succotash

Serves 8

¼ cup olive or vegetable oil

1 large clove garlic, crushed

1 pound zucchini, diced

4 ears of corn, kernels cut

8 scallions, chopped (including tops)

2 chili peppers (Anaheim, mild) seeds removed and chopped

1 small green bell pepper, diced

1 small red bell pepper, diced (or 1 can pimiento)

2 teaspoons salt

1 teaspoon pepper

2 tomatoes, peeled, seeded, and diced

- In a heavy skillet, heat olive oil and garlic over moderately low heat for 5 minutes. Remove and discard the garlic. Add zucchini, corn, scallions, green chilies, green pepper and red pepper. Sprinkle with salt and pepper and simmer, covered, over low heat for 15 minutes or until the flavors are well blended and the vegetables are tender but still crisp. Top the mixture with the tomatoes and cook, covered, for 1 more minute.

Note: This may be prepared ahead and reheated briefly before serving. A good accompaniment to any Mexican food, barbecued meats or roasts.

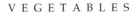

Apricot Wild Rice

Serves 6

3 cups cooked wild rice

4 tablespoons melted butter

4 tablespoons chopped parsley

2 tablespoons chopped onion

¾ cup chopped celery leaves

¾ cup chopped dried apricots

⅛ teaspoon dried thyme

⅛ teaspoon mace

⅛ teaspoon freshly grated nutmeg

⅛ teaspoon ground cloves

1 teaspoon freshly ground black pepper

½ teaspoon salt

- While rice is cooking, melt butter in a small skillet and sauté the onion until translucent, add parsley and celery leaves and apricots.

- While rice is still hot, combine with all ingredients, toss and serve warm.

Aunt Fanny's Baked Squash

Serves 6

3 pounds yellow summer squash, coarsely chopped (or any squash)

½ cup chopped onion

½ cup dry breadcrumbs (cracker crumbs may be used)

1 teaspoon salt

½ teaspoon freshly ground black pepper

2 eggs, well beaten

1 tablespoon granulated sugar

½ cup butter, melted

- In a large pot of boiling water, cook squash until tender; drain and mash (purée).

- To the squash, add the onion, breadcrumbs, salt, pepper, eggs, sugar and ¼ cup melted butter.

- Pour squash mixture into a baking dish. Pour the remaining ¼ cup melted butter over the top and sprinkle with the bread or cracker crumbs.

- Bake in a 375° oven for about 45 minutes to 1 hour or until brown on top.

Acorn Squash with Applesauce

Serves 4

2 medium-sized acorn squash

1 teaspoon safflower oil

2 cups applesauce, preferably homemade

½ teaspoon cinnamon

2 tablespoons apple juice concentrate

¼ cup raisins

- Cut the squash in half, and trim a flat edge on the rounded side so the squash will not tilt when filled. Scoop the seeds and extra fiber from the squash. Rub the cut side and the cavity with the oil. Oil a baking sheet and place the squash, cut side down, on the sheet. Bake at 350° for 45 minutes.

- Combine the applesauce, cinnamon, apple juice and raisins. Remove the squash from the oven, turn cavity side up. Spoon the applesauce mixture into the cavities. Return to the oven and bake for an additional 20 minutes, until piping hot.

John Randolph's Yam Loaf

Serves 6

2 tablespoons butter

1 small onion, chopped (about ¼ cup)

1 tablespoon flour

½ teaspoon salt

⅛ teaspoon pepper

1 cup milk

1 cup soft breadcrumbs

1 cup pecans, finely chopped

2 cups cooked mashed sweet potatoes

- Melt the butter in a cast iron skillet and brown the onion. Stir in the flour, salt and pepper. Add the milk and simmer until the mixture becomes thick. Add the breadcrumbs, nuts and sweet potatoes. Blend thoroughly.

- Preheat oven to 350°. Place the skillet, filled with the sweet potato mixture, in the oven and bake for 30 minutes or until nicely browned. Serve while hot, or split when cold and toast.

Note: Indian yam cakes are made by shaping the mixture into small balls, flattening them slightly on a baking sheet. Bake in a 425° oven for 10 to 20 minutes.

Kentucky Fresh Corn Pudding

Serves 8

6 ears of sweet corn on the cob

6 whole eggs, stirred not beaten

3 cups heavy cream

½ cup granulated sugar

1 teaspoon salt

1 teaspoon flour

½ teaspoon baking powder

2 teaspoons butter, melted

- Prepare the corn by using a sharp knife to barely cut through the center of the kernels down the row on the cob. Then, using the back side of a kitchen knife, scrape the cob to remove the corn juice and pulp. There should be about 3 cups of corn pulp.

- Combine the corn pulp with the eggs and cream.

- Mix sugar, salt, flour and baking powder. Add to the corn pulp, stir in the melted butter, and mix well.

- Butter a 6-cup baking dish. Pour in the pudding mixture and bake at 350° for about 1 hour, or until a knife inserted in the center comes out clean.

Beulah Mae's Creole Baked Eggplant

Serves 6

1 large eggplant

1 cup chopped celery

1 cup chopped green pepper

2 large tomatoes, chopped

1 bunch scallions, chopped

½ cup soft breadcrumbs

2 beaten eggs

1 teaspoon salt

Freshly ground black pepper

4 tablespoons butter

1½ cups grated cheese (Mozzarella or Swiss cheese)

- Peel, slice and cube eggplant. In a medium saucepan, bring about 2 inches of water to a boil. Cook eggplant in the water just until tender; drain.

- In the same saucepan (adding more water if necessary), cook the remaining vegetables separately; drain.

- Combine cooked vegetables with the breadcrumbs, eggs, salt and pepper. Pour into a greased ovenproof casserole. Dot the top with butter and top with cheese.

- Bake casserole in a 350° oven for 30 minutes.

121

Eggplant Rolls

Serves 6

   2 large eggplants

   Olive oil

   1½ cups ricotta cheese

   ¾ cup freshly grated Parmesan cheese

   1½ cups cheese, grated Swiss or mozzarella

   ¾ cup sour cream (or nonfat yogurt)

   1 to 2 teaspoons horseradish

   Salt

   Freshly ground black pepper

Fresh Tomato Sauce:

   6 large ripe tomatoes

   4 tablespoons olive oil

   2 garlic cloves, finely chopped

   Salt and freshly ground black pepper

   1 tablespoon chopped fresh parsley leaves, or
      mixture of parsley, basil and oregano leaves

- Preheat oven to 350°.

- Slice the eggplant lengthwise in ¼-inch slices. Place on a baking sheet and brush with olive oil and bake for 20 minutes. Turn over and brush with olive oil. Bake for 10 minutes. Slices should be soft and pliable.

- Mix together the cheeses, sour cream, horseradish, salt and pepper. Spread cheese filling on eggplant slices. Roll slices, starting with the narrow end, and place in an ovenproof baking dish. Top with a fresh tomato sauce and bake in preheated oven for 15 to 18 minutes.

• • •

- Peel, seed and dice the tomatoes; place in a sieve to drain off excess juices. Let set for 10 minutes.

- In a medium skillet or saucepan, heat the oil and sauté the garlic just until it begins to color. Add the tomatoes and season with salt and pepper. Cook over high heat, uncovered, for 7 to 8 minutes, or until the tomatoes lose their excess juices. Stir in the herbs.

Note: This basic tomato sauce is also used for any dried pasta, such as spaghetti, ziti, penne or shells.

Gratin Monegasque (Gratin Monaco-style)

Serves 6

2 pounds zucchini, thickly sliced

2 pounds eggplant, peeled and thickly sliced

2 pounds ripe tomatoes, thickly sliced

1½ pounds onions, peeled and sliced

2 large cloves of garlic, chopped

½ cup olive oil

Salt and freshly ground black pepper

1 teaspoon fresh thyme (½ teaspoon dried)

1 teaspoon fresh oregano (½ teaspoon dried)

- Put the zucchini, eggplant and tomatoes in an oiled gratin dish, and place the onions and garlic on top. Drizzle olive oil over the top of the vegetables, and sprinkle with salt, pepper, thyme and oregano.

- Bake in a 400° oven for 1 hour. (Check for doneness at 30 minutes, and adjust time accordingly.)

Simca's Vegetable Clafouti

A traditional clafouti (or clafoutis) is a simple cherry dessert of fresh fruit covered with a pancake batter and baked in a fireproof dish. This is a most unusual variation similar to a crustless quiche.

Serves 6

1 10-inch porcelain fluted pie plate

⅔ cup toasted breadcrumbs

2½ tablespoons creamed butter

1 pound tender leeks (or zucchini)

4 tablespoons vegetable oil

3 ounces Roquefort cheese

1 cup crème fraîche

1 pound cream cheese

4 eggs

Salt and freshly ground white pepper

1 tablespoon "Herbs de Provence" (dry thyme, marjoram, oregano and savory)

1 tablespoon minced fresh chives

- Smear the butter on the pie plate, more on the sides. Press the breadcrumbs into the butter and let it set in the refrigerator.

- Clean the leeks (if using zucchini, do not peel), chop the leeks using only the tender part, both green and white (if using zucchini, slice thin).

- In a heavy pan, heat the oil, add the leeks (or zucchini) and let them stew slowly, stirring constantly until tender. Season with salt and pepper. (40 to 45 minutes for leeks, 20 to 25 minutes for zucchini.)

- Crumble the Roquefort with a fork. Then, using a food processor, pulse the Roquefort with ¾ cup crème fraîche (reserve the other ¼ cup for later). Add the cream cheese, then the eggs and all the seasonings; combine with the leeks.

- Pour the mixture into the prepared pie plate. Bake in a preheated 350° oven for about 25 minutes, the center should be set.

Note: If you prepare ahead, bake only 20 minutes. Then smear the remaining crème fraîche over the top and put back in the oven for 10 more minutes to nicely brown the top.

Note: For a Mushroom Clafouti, use 1 pound fresh, washed, sliced mushrooms instead of the leeks or zucchini. Wild mushrooms may also be used.

Stir-Fry Summer Squash Medley

Serves 4 to 6

1 tablespoon vegetable oil

1 zucchini, cut into strips ½" x 1½"

2 summer squash, cut into ½" cubes

1 yellow crookneck or yellow Italian squash, cut on diagonal (the larger diagonal slices should be cut in half)

1 red bell pepper, seeded and cut into ¼" x 1" strips

1 thinly sliced scallion, sliced on the diagonal

⅓ cup minced fresh dill

1½ tablespoons freshly squeezed lemon juice

1 teaspoon grated lemon zest

¼ teaspoon crushed red pepper flakes or ⅛ teaspoon cayenne (optional)

- Heat wok, or large skillet, until very hot. Add the oil. Watch carefully and as soon as the oil begins to smoke, add the squash, and stir-fry 6 minutes.

- Add peppers and scallions, and continue to stir-fry another 3 minutes.

- Add the dill, lemon juice, lemon zest and red pepper if you choose. Toss to coat the vegetables and stir-fry 1 more minute. Serve immediately.

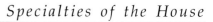

Southern-Style Carrots

Serves 4 to 6

3 cups peeled and thinly sliced carrots (about 8 medium)

½ cup minced onion

½ cup mayonnaise

1 to 2 tablespoons grated horseradish

½ teaspoon salt

¼ teaspoon freshly ground black pepper

1 slice bread

1 tablespoon butter, softened

¼ teaspoon paprika

- Preheat oven to 375°.

- Bring 2 cups of water to a boil in a medium saucepan. Add the carrots and cook for 5 to 6 minutes. Drain, reserving ¼ cup cooking liquid.

- Butter a shallow 1½-quart casserole. Place the carrots in the casserole.

- Combine the reserved cooking liquid with the onion, mayonnaise, horseradish, salt and pepper. Spoon over the top of the carrots.

- Butter the slice of bread and sprinkle with paprika. Whirl the bread in the food processor until crumbly. Sprinkle the breadcrumbs over the top of the carrot mixture. Bake, in the preheated oven, uncovered, for 20 to 25 minutes.

Note: This dish may be prepared early in the day and baked just before serving.

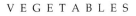
Beets, Onions and Apples

Serves 6 to 8

2½ pounds fresh beets (approximately)

¼ cup rice vinegar

1 tart green apple

1 tablespoon butter

1 red onion, thinly sliced

1 clove garlic, minced

1 teaspoon minced fresh ginger root

¾ cup rice vinegar

1 cup sugar

3 tablespoons cornstarch

3 tablespoons cold water

Salt

Freshly ground white pepper

- Cut tops from the beets, leaving about 2 inches of stem. Discard the tops. Leave the roots attached and scrub the beets well. Place the beets in a large pan and cover with water. Add ¼ cup rice vinegar. Bring to a boil, reduce heat and simmer beets until tender, about 45 minutes.

- Drain beets, reserving 1 cup cooking liquid. Run beets under cold water. Slip off the skins. Cut off the beet tops and roots, and slice ¼-inch thick. Set aside.

- Core apple and cut into thin lengthwise slices.

- In a large skillet, melt the butter, add the apple, onion, garlic and ginger. Sauté until apple and onion are tender. Stir in remaining ¾ cup vinegar, sugar and reserved beet liquid. Heat to simmer.

- Blend cornstarch and water, stir until smooth. Add to the skillet and cook, stirring gently, until mixture is thickened and becomes clear. Carefully stir in the beets to coat with the sauce. When the beets are warmed through, serve.

Note: This is a delicious side dish for any pork chop or pork roast preparation.

Thai Green Beans

Serves 4

½ pound fresh green beans

1 teaspoon vegetable oil

1 cup sliced fresh mushrooms

3 cloves garlic, minced

3 tablespoons cold water

1½ teaspoons cornstarch

2 green onions, cut into 1½-inch pieces

1 tablespoon soy sauce

¼ teaspoon black pepper, freshly ground*

2 tablespoons coarsely chopped unsalted, dry-
roasted peanuts

1 tablespoon coarsely chopped fresh cilantro

- Wash beans. Trim ends and remove strings. Cut in half and set aside. (If you are using baby green beans, leave them whole.)

- In a medium skillet, over high heat, sauté the garlic for about 30 seconds. Add the mushrooms, sauté for about 30 seconds more. Reduce heat to medium, add the green beans, and cook 3 to 5 minutes, or until crisp-tender, tossing frequently for even cooking.

- In a small bowl, combine water and cornstarch, stir well. To the mixture in the skillet, add the cornstarch mixture, green onions, soy sauce and pepper. Cook 2 minutes, stirring constantly, until thickened and the beans are coated with the sauce. Remove from heat, sprinkle with peanuts and cilantro. Serve warm.

*Crushed red pepper flakes can be substituted for the black pepper for extra zing!

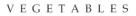
Spaghetti Squash au Gratin

1 2-pound spaghetti squash

2 tablespoons chopped fresh marjoram or ½ teaspoon dried

¼ teaspoon freshly ground white pepper

Pinch of salt

6 tablespoons freshly grated Parmesan cheese

- Place a couple of inches of water in a deep pot, insert a vegetable steamer, and bring to boil over high heat. Cut the squash into quarters and scrape out the seeds. Place the quarters in the steamer flesh side down and steam for 20 to 30 minutes or until your finger leaves an impression on the shell.

- Remove from the steam and, when cool enough to handle, take a table fork and gently "comb" the squash lengthwise into a mixing bowl. The strands will fall into your bowl like pieces of spaghetti.

- Preheat broiler. Combine the squash with the marjoram, pepper and salt. Place in a 1-quart baking dish and sprinkle with Parmesan cheese. Place under the broiler for 2 minutes and serve immediately.

"Tis an ill cook that cannot lick his own fingers."

Shakespeare (1564-1616)

Seafood

The probate inventory of 1782 and the estate sale of 1798 list "Queens Chinia," or cream-colored ware, among the Lewis' belongings. This creamware grand platt menage, circa 1780-1795, features the figure of Plenty above two tiers of shells meant to hold sweetmeats, such as glazed fruits, nuts and comfits.

Crayfish Étouffee

Serves 4 to 6

½ cup butter

2 large onions, minced

1 rib celery, minced

2 garlic cloves, minced

2 medium green bell peppers, minced

1 tablespoon flour

2 pounds crayfish tails

Crayfish fat

Salt and freshly ground black pepper

Dash of cayenne pepper

1 cup hot water

½ cup chopped green onion tops

½ cup chopped parsley

- In a medium skillet, melt butter over low heat and cook onions, celery, garlic and green pepper until golden brown, about 30 minutes.

- Add 1 tablespoon flour to the skillet, stir thoroughly, and cook the roux (the butter-flour mixture) for 1 to 2 minutes. Add the crayfish tails and crayfish fat. Season with salt, black pepper and cayenne pepper. Add 1 cup hot water for desired thickness of the gravy. Let simmer in covered pot until tails are tender.

- At serving time, sprinkle onion tops and parsley over the étouffee. Serve over hot white rice.

Baltimore Crab Cakes

Serves 8

5 pounds finest quality lump crabmeat

½ teaspoon salt

1 tablespoon freshly ground black pepper

1 tablespoon Old Bay seasoning

5 eggs

5 tablespoons mayonnaise (or more to bind)

6 tablespoons Dijon-style mustard

1½ cups crushed saltine crackers

Worcestershire sauce

- Preheat oven to broil.

- On a large flat pan, spread crabmeat evenly. Sprinkle the salt, pepper, Old Bay and crackers over the crabmeat.

- Add eggs, mayonnaise and mustard to crabmeat; spritz generously with Worcestershire sauce. Mix thoroughly but lightly by hand. Form into 16 crab cakes.

- Broil the crab cakes 4 or 5 inches from the flame until golden brown (about 3 minutes).

Note: Prepare 2 crab cakes per person. Serve with coleslaw and saltines (plain) or French bread (fancy). Beer is best either way. Cocktail or tartar sauce is not appropriate with these crab cakes.

Natchez Deviled Oysters

Serves 12

2 quarts fresh oysters

½ cup butter

1 cup finely chopped celery

1 tablespoon flour

1 cup milk

½ teaspoon fresh thyme (¼ teaspoon dried)

Dash of liquid red pepper seasoning

Dash of Worcestershire sauce

4 to 6 cups saltine cracker crumbs

¼ cup butter

- Preheat oven to 400°.

- Drain oysters reserving the oyster liquor. Strain the liquor in a fine mesh sieve to remove any shell particles. Chop oysters, if very large, set aside.

- Melt butter in large saucepan, add celery and sauté until limp. Add the oysters.

- Whisk together the flour and milk; add slowly to the oyster mixture, stirring constantly. Add ¼ cup of the oyster liquor. Add seasonings.

- Stir all but 1 cup of the cracker crumbs into the oyster mixture. Set aside 1 cup crumbs for topping.

- Lightly butter a 3-quart baking dish. Pour oyster mixture into the prepared dish, and top with a thin layer of cracker crumbs and dot with butter.

- Put oysters into preheated oven and bake for 30 minutes or until brown.

Note: As a first course, this is served on individual plates; or, it can be baked on individual scallop shells or in individual ramekins.

Shreveport Oysters

Serves 8 as a first course, more from a chafing dish as an appetizer

4 ribs celery, chopped (about ½ pound)

4 bunches scallions, chopped (about 1 pound)

3 large cloves garlic, chopped

1¼ cups butter, melted

2 cups cooked spinach, chopped and squeezed dry

4 tablespoons chopped parsley

2 teaspoons salt

⅛ teaspoon cayenne

½ teaspoon ground anise seed (¼ cup Herbsaint, absinthe)

1 tablespoon freshly squeezed lemon juice

3 tablespoons Worcestershire sauce

3 tablespoons catsup

2 ounces anchovy fillets, mashed to a paste

Breadcrumbs, unseasoned, as needed

4 dozen freshly shucked oysters with liquor

- In a large skillet, melt butter and sauté celery, scallions and garlic for 5 minutes. Remove from heat, and add spinach, parsley and seasonings.

- In a food processor or blender (in batches if necessary), purée the spinach mixture. Thicken with breadcrumbs to make a dense sauce.

- Drain oysters, pick them over to remove any shell fragments. Strain the liquor in a fine mesh sieve, reserve. Place oysters in a shallow layer in a shallow baking pan. Pour the oyster liquor over the oysters, and poach in a 400° oven just until curled, about 5 or 6 minutes.

- To serve from a chafing dish: Reheat sauce in a saucepan. Using a slotted spoon, transfer oysters to the chafing dish and combine with warm sauce. Serve with plain melba toast rounds or thinly sliced French bread.

- To serve as a first course: Heat plates and spoon sauce onto the plates, with slotted spoon serve oysters on the spinach sauce. Sprinkle with additional parsley.

Note: This recipe is a tradition on Christmas Eve in Shreveport, Louisiana.

Gamberoni Al Forno
(Mediterranean Jumbo Shrimp)

Serves 4 to 6

2 pounds raw jumbo shrimp, in shells

¾ cup extra virgin olive oil

½ cup sweet Marsala

½ cup fresh lemon juice

4 garlic cloves, minced

4 scallions, minced

Salt and freshly ground black pepper to taste

4 tablespoons minced fresh oregano (2 tablespoons dried)

Fresh mint sprigs

- Preheat oven to 425°.

- Cut shrimp down the back and remove the vein. Do not remove the shell. Place shrimp in a shallow baking dish. Add remaining ingredients except oregano and mint. Bake 10 minutes, basting occasionally.

- Mix oregano with pan juices and baste again. Continue baking until shrimp just turns a bright pink, about 3 minutes more. Do not overcook.

- Transfer shrimp to a serving dish and garnish with mint. Serve with crusty bread to soak up the succulent sauce.

Shrimp in Cabbage Leaves with Caviar

Serves 8

8 large cabbage leaves

24 medium raw shrimp, with shells

2 tablespoons olive oil

Salt and freshly ground black pepper

3 tablespoons clam juice

3 tablespoons wine vinegar

¾ cup butter, softened

2 ounces black caviar (the best you can afford)
(do not use pressed caviar for this recipe)

- Preheat oven to 350°.

- In a large pot filled with salted water, cook cabbage leaves about 8 minutes, or until wilted. Lift the leaves from the water, cool in cold water and drain on paper towels to dry.

- In the same pot of boiling water, plunge the shrimp and cook only until opaque; do not overcook. Cool shrimp; shell and devein.

- Spread the large cabbage leaves, place 3 shrimps on each leaf, salt and pepper to taste; roll up the cabbage leaves folding in sides to seal.

- In an ovenproof casserole, pour 2 tablespoons olive oil, carefully place filled cabbage leaves. Cover and bake about 15 minutes at 350°, or until heated through.

- In the meantime, in a heavy saucepan combine clam juice, vinegar and shallots, boil to reduce to 1 tablespoon. Strain liquid and return to the saucepan. Add butter in small amounts whisking rapidly to incorporate the butter into the liquid. Fold in caviar.

- Place 1 cabbage roll on each plate and top with caviar butter sauce.

Shrimp and Lobster Perditas

This recipe from Perditas' Restaurant in Charleston, South Carolina, is for one serving.
It is easily duplicated to make individual servings for as many as you invite.

Serves 1

¼ **pound cooked shrimp**

¼ **pound cooked lobster meat, diced**

2 **thin slices lemon**

2 **tablespoons butter**

1 **teaspoon chopped parsley**

Dash of freshly grated nutmeg

Dash of salt

2 **crushed peppercorns**

Dash of paprika

2-inch **block of sharp Cheddar cheese**

1 **tablespoon good dry sherry**

Mustard Sauce:

1 **teaspoon Dijon-style mustard**

¼ **teaspoon fresh lemon juice**

½ **cup heavy cream**

½ **cup Chablis wine (Chenin Blanc or Sauvignon Blanc are good substitutes)**

- Cut a piece of heavy aluminum foil 10" x 12". On the foil, place the shrimp, cut in halves, and the lobster. Add lemon slices, butter, parsley, nutmeg, salt, crushed pepper and paprika.

- In a small saucepan (or in the microwave) melt the Cheddar cheese and stir in the sherry. Pour over the shellfish.

•   •   •

- Make the mustard sauce by whisking all 4 ingredients together. Pour over the shellfish.

- Fold the foil over the shrimp mixture in a drug-store wrap; it must be a completely leakproof rectangular package. Preheat oven to 375°. Place foil packages on a baking sheet and heat for 10 to 15 minutes. (If you have prepared ahead and refrigerated, heat for 30 minutes.)

- To serve: Place the foil package on a plate. Make two horizontal cuts on the long side of the rectangle, (do not cut all the way through) and lift this "handle" for the foil basket. Guests should eat directly from the foil basket. Serve with French bread and green salad.

Cushing's Shrimp Fantasy

Serves 4

1 cup peanut oil

½ cup flaked coconut

⅓ cup dry breadcrumbs

3 tablespoons parsley

1 tablespoon minced garlic

1 teaspoon salt

¼ teaspoon freshly ground black pepper

½ teaspoon paprika

2 pounds raw medium shrimp

⅔ cup dry sherry

- Preheat oven to 375°.

- Mix together the peanut oil, coconut, breadcrumbs, parsley, garlic, salt, pepper and paprika. Set aside a third of this mixture as a topping.

- Add the shrimp to the bowl and toss to coat the shrimp. Put the shrimp into a lightly buttered 1½-quart casserole or baking pan. Pour the sherry over the shrimp and top with the reserved coconut topping.

- Bake, uncovered, in the preheated oven for 30 to 40 minutes. (Be careful not to overcook or the shrimp will toughen.)

Note: William Barker Cushing (1843-1900) was an eminent naval officer during the Civil War. He was a midwesterner who became famous in his time and then forgotten with the passage of time.

Shrimp & Grits, Crook's Corner Style

Serves 4

1 teaspoon salt

1 cup hominy grits

1 teaspoon butter

¼ to ¾ cup grated sharp Cheddar cheese

Hot pepper sauce

Freshly grated nutmeg

White pepper, freshly ground

3 slices bacon, diced

1 pound medium shrimp, peeled, deveined, rinsed and patted dry

2 cups sliced mushrooms

1 cup finely sliced scallions

1 large garlic clove, peeled and minced

2 tablespoons chopped fresh parsley

4 teaspoons lemon juice

Salt and freshly ground black pepper

- In a heavy 3-quart saucepan, combine 4½ cups water and salt; bring to a boil. Slowly sift grits through one hand into the water, stirring with a whisk in the other hand. When all grits have been added, continue stirring and reduce heat to very low, until only an occasional bubble breaks the surface. Continue cooking for 30 to 40 minutes, stirring frequently to prevent scorching.

- Beat in the butter and cheese. Season to taste with hot pepper sauce, a very little nutmeg and white pepper. Cover and hold in a warm place or in the top of a double boiler over simmering water.

- Sauté bacon lightly over medium-high heat in a medium skillet. The bacon should not become too crisp. Remove bacon, discard fat and return the bacon to the skillet.

- When the skillet is hot, add the shrimp in an even layer. Turn shrimp as they begin to color, add mushrooms and sauté 2 to 4 minutes, until shrimp are pink and just firm.

- Stir in scallions and garlic. Season with lemon juice, parsley and hot pepper sauce. Add salt and pepper to taste.

- Divide grits among 4 warm plates. Spoon shrimp over them and serve.

Note: Crook's Corner is a restaurant in Chapel Hill, North Carolina owned and operated by Bill Neal.

Pecan-Coated Catfish

Serves 4

2 pounds freshwater catfish fillets

Unbleached white flour

⅔ cup finely chopped pecans

⅔ cup cracker or dry breadcrumbs

2 eggs

½ cup milk

2 teaspoons Dijon-style mustard

Salt

Freshly ground black pepper

2 tablespoons butter

2 tablespoons vegetable oil

2 tablespoons dry white wine

Lemon wedges for garnish

- Dredge the fish in flour.

- In a large shallow bowl, whisk the eggs, milk and mustard until combined.

- Mix pecans with crumbs and spread on a plate. Dip the flour-coated fillets in the egg mixture then in the pecan mixture. Sprinkle with salt and plenty of freshly ground black pepper. Place the fillets on a sheet of waxed paper and refrigerate for 15 minutes for the coating to set.

- In a large, heavy skillet, heat to a moderate temperature and add the butter and oil. When the butter starts to foam, add the fish fillets. Sauté fillets until golden, about 2 minutes on each side. Reduce heat to moderately-low, add the wine and cover the skillet. Cook just until fish flakes easily, about 2 to 3 minutes. Serve immediately, garnished with lemon wedges.

Mussels with Chili Vinaigrette

Serves 6 as appetizers

Chili Vinaigrette:
- ½ **cup cider vinegar**
- 1 **shallot, minced**
- 1 **teaspoon Dijon-style mustard**
- 1 **teaspoon Worcestershire sauce**
- **Salt and freshly ground black pepper**
- 1 **cup virgin olive oil**
- ½ **jalapeño chili, minced with a few of its seeds**
- ½ **small red bell pepper, diced**
- ½ **tablespoon olive oil**
- ¼ **cup chopped parsley leaves (Italian parsley if possible)**
- 1 **small bunch cilantro leaves, chopped**
- 1 **bunch baby spinach leaves or watercress leaves**

The Mussels:
- 3 **pounds medium fresh mussels**
- 1 **cup white wine (a Reisling is good)**
- 3 **bay leaves**
- 3 **shallots, roughly chopped**
- 1 **teaspoon whole black peppercorns**
- 1 **small leek, julienned**

- Combine vinegar, shallot, mustard, Worcestershire sauce, salt and pepper in a small bowl. Whisk in the oil slowly.

- In a small skillet, sauté the minced jalapeño and red bell pepper in olive oil for 2 to 3 minutes.

- Combine the vinegar mixture with the sautéed peppers. Add the parsley and cilantro. Allow to stand for about 1 hour. Stir again and correct the seasoning. (If desired, you may increase the chili "heat" by adding extra jalapeño peppers, but be careful!)

     •   •   •

- Wash mussels thoroughly in cold water. Discard any mussels that are open. A gentle tap may cause some to close, those are fine. Scrub the shells and remove the "beards".

- In a large sauté pan with a close fitting lid, combine white wine, bay leaves, shallots and black peppercorns. Simmer for 5 minutes. Add the mussels and increase to high heat. Boil with the lid on until the mussels open, about 5 minutes. Add the leeks and cook for 30 seconds more. (If some shells don't open, cook these a little longer. Discard any still unopened mussels.)

     •   •   •

Continued on next page

Continued from previous page

Note:The chili vinaigrette is a wonderful dressing for grilled chicken, fish or shellfish. This recipe was the inspiration of Chef John Downey, Downey's Restaurant, Santa Barbara, California.

To Serve:

- Wash 1 bunch of tiny spinach leaves or watercress.

- Carefully remove the mussels from their shells. If sand is present, wash both the shells and the mussels.

- Arrange the half-shells on a plate like the spokes of a wheel. Place a tiny spinach leaf in each shell, then place a mussel on top. Spoon the chili vinaigrette generously over the mussel. Garnish with the cilantro.

Baked Fish with Walnut-Coriander Chutney

Serves 6

1½ cups coriander leaves (cilantro)

¾ cup English walnut pieces

5 tablespoons lemon juice

3 cloves garlic, coarsely chopped

1 jalapeño pepper, seeded and coarsely chopped

Salt, to taste

6 pieces swordfish, tuna, or rock cod (about 6 ounces each)

Walnut pieces, toasted

- Preheat oven to 400°.

- In a blender, combine coriander, ¾ cup walnut pieces, lemon juice, garlic and jalapeño. Blend to make a rough paste, pulsing blender on and off and scraping sides, as needed. Mix in salt.

- Arrange fish in a shallow baking pan. Spread walnut mixture on fish. Bake in the preheated 400° oven just until fish is opaque, 5 to 10 minutes (depending on thickness of fish).

- Garnish with toasted walnuts. Serve with roasted potatoes.

Note: This recipe is attributed to Joyce Goldstein, chef/owner of Square One restaurant in San Francisco.

Salmon Papillotes with Lime Sauce

Serves 2

1 salmon fillet (about ¾ pound) cut from the center

2½ tablespoons butter

Salt and freshly ground black pepper

1 pinch cayenne pepper

Scant ½ teaspoon grated ginger root

1 lime

1 small shallot

1½ tablespoons port, plus a few drops for finishing

1½ tablespoons heavy cream

- Cut the salmon fillet in half horizontally with a thin sharp knife.

- Cut 2 feet from a roll of parchment paper. Round off the corners to make an oval about 24" x 15". Fold in half crosswise and open it again. Butter half the paper from the fold to within 1½-inches of the edge, using 1 teaspoon of the butter; this will become the inside of the papillote.

- Put the salmon slices side by side on the buttered part of the paper and season with salt and pepper, pinch of cayenne and the grated ginger. Grate the zest from a quarter of the lime over the fillets and sprinkle with a few drops of lime juice.

- Fold the parchment paper over the fish. Don't let the paper stick to the top of the fish and try to enclose as much air as possible when you seal the papillote. Roll the edges and then press flat, making a sealed hem. Put the papillote on a baking sheet and set aside.

•   •   •

- Chop the shallot and squeeze 2 tablespoons lime juice. In a small pan, soften the chopped shallot by cooking it in 2 teaspoons of the butter over low heat. Add the lime juice and port and reduce the liquid by half over high heat.

- Preheat oven to 500°. (Finish the sauce before baking the papillotes.) To finish the sauce, reheat the port and lime mixture, add cream and bring to a boil. Over low heat, whisk into the sauce the remaining

Continued on next page

Continued from previous page

1½ tablespoons butter. Season with salt and pepper and a pinch of cayenne. Just before serving, add a few drops of port wine and perhaps a little more grated ginger.

- Put the papillote in the preheated oven and bake for just 3 minutes. Serve immediately with sauce.

Note: With port, ginger, lime juice and salmon, this recipe reflects the homogeneity of international cooking. Surprisingly, this recipe comes from Fredy Girardet, Crissier, Switzerland. His restaurant is often labeled "The Finest Restaurant in the World".

Priceless Filet of Sole

Serves 4 to 6

2 pounds sole
1 tablespoon white wine vinegar
1 tablespoon Worcestershire sauce
1 tablespoon lemon juice
1 teaspoon Dijon-style mustard
1 teaspoon salt
½ teaspoon freshly ground black pepper
½ cup butter, melted

- Mix together the vinegar, Worcestershire sauce, lemon juice, mustard, salt and pepper and butter to make a smooth spread.

- Butter an ovenproof casserole dish. Sprinkle with breadcrumbs, layer the sole then the sauce. Sprinkle with paprika. Bake in a 400° oven for 20 minutes.

Grilled Shark with Anchovy-Parsley Paste

Serves 4

1 cup fresh parsley

2 cloves garlic

1 tin anchovies in olive oil

½ cup olive oil

4 shark steaks

Salt and freshly ground pepper

2 tablespoons olive oil

- In food processor, combine parsley, garlic and anchovies. Purée until smooth. Add ½ cup olive oil and process to a smooth paste.

- Heat grill to high temperature. Sprinkle shark with salt and pepper, and drizzle with olive oil. Grill 3 to 5 minutes on each side, depending on thickness of the shark steaks. After turning the steaks, spread the anchovy-parsley paste on shark. Continue cooking, but do not overcook.

Grilled Red Snapper with Citrus Melange

Serves 4

1 garlic clove

1 small shallot

1 medium lemon

1 medium lime

1 medium orange

1 small red grapefruit

2 small tomatoes

1½ pounds red snapper (4 fillets)

4 tablespoons olive oil

1 teaspoon salt

½ teaspoon freshly ground black pepper

3 tablespoons julienned basil leaves

4 basil leaves reserved for garnish

- Peel and mince the garlic and shallot, set aside.

- Peel and section the citrus fruits. Place fruits in a glass bowl. Peel, seed, and chop the tomatoes. Combine with the citrus.

- Preheat the grill or broiler.* Brush the fillets with 2 tablespoons olive oil. Season with salt and pepper. Grill or broil the fish until just cooked, about 3 minutes per side. Remove from heat, cover and keep warm.

- In a medium saucepan, or skillet, heat the remaining 2 tablespoons olive oil. Sauté the garlic and shallots until softened, about 1 minute. Add the citrus-tomato mixture, julienned basil, salt and pepper. Warm over low heat for 2 minutes. Adjust the seasonings. (Be careful not to heat the sauce too much or the fruit sections will lose their shape.)

- Transfer fish to 4 warm dinner plates. Spoon the sauce over the fish. Garnish with the reserved basil leaves and serve immediately.

*The fish can also be quickly sautéed in a nonstick skillet.

*"No man can be wise on
an empty stomach."*

George Eliot

Poultry

During school tours at Kenmore, young students search for egg cups and then recite "Humpty Dumpty sat in a spoon" when they find the objects names in the nursery rhyme. Here in the first-floor chamber of Kenmore, students learn that the colonists sometimes ate their meals in their bedchambers.

Smothered Doves

Serves 4

12 doves

Butter

Salt and pepper

Flour

6 tablespoons Worcestershire sauce

6 slices bacon

- Clean doves well. Rub breasts with a little butter. Sprinkle well inside and out with salt, pepper and flour. If split down the back, pull sides together to appear as if uncut. Place breast side down in a shallow baking dish or a very small roasting pan.

- Sprinkle with Worcestershire sauce and lay a half slice of bacon on each bird. Add enough water to half cover. Bake at 450° for 25 minutes. Reduce heat to 400° and continue to cook for about 45 minutes, or until very tender, depending upon age of birds. Add water, if needed, during cooking to keep from getting too dry.

Grilled Duck Breast
with Blackberry, Cassis and Sage Sauce

Serves 4

2 duck breasts, boned and split, trimmed of fat

Marinade:

½ **cup finely chopped carrots**

½ **cup finely chopped celery**

½ **cup finely chopped onions**

Grated rind of 1 lime

1 large garlic clove, finely minced

¼ **cup olive oil**

Sauce:

3 tablespoons chopped shallots

3 tablespoons blackberry vinegar (plus more to taste)

⅓ **cup cassis (plus more to taste)**

1 cup freshly squeezed orange juice

1 cup dry white wine

1½ cups brown duck demi-glace (commercially prepared or made in the kitchen from a standard reduced brown duck stock recipe)

1 teaspoon chopped fresh sage

1½ teaspoons blackberry purée

4 tablespoons heavy cream

1 tablespoon butter

Salt and freshly ground pepper to taste

- Mix marinade mixture and slather mixture on duck breasts. Let marinate for 1 hour.

• • •

- For the sauce: In a saucepan heat the shallots, blackberry vinegar and cassis. Bring to a simmer, add orange juice and reduce by half. Add white wine, reduce by half. Add more cassis or vinegar to taste. Add brown duck demi-glace and sage. Reduce mixture by one third, skimming frequently. Strain. Return liquid to saucepan (there should be about 1½ cups), bring to a simmer. Add a pinch of sage, blackberry purée, cream and butter. Reduce until sauce thickens. Salt and pepper to taste.

- Rub marinade off duck breasts, then brush with olive oil and grill breasts, fat side down, over hot grill for 4 minutes. After 2 minutes, rotate breasts to get a cross-hatch pattern and insure even cooking. Brush flesh with olive oil and flip. Grill for 4 more minutes repeating the rotation for cross hatching. Duck breasts should feel firm. (This time is for rare to medium. For more doneness add 2 minutes on each side.) Remove from grill, let rest 4 minutes skin side down in a warm place.

- Slice on the bias and place skin side up on a small pool of sauce on the plate. Fan out slices and pour additional sauce around edges. Lightly salt.

151

Wild Goose Steaks

Serves 4

2 wild goose breasts

4 tablespoons butter

Salt and freshly ground pepper

- Bone and skin goose breasts. Lay flat on a cutting board and cut in half horizontally. If goose is large you can make 3 pieces from each breast. Pieces should be about the thickness of calves liver.

- Heat a large, heavy skillet (preferably cast iron) over high heat. Skillet should be very hot and dry. Place 4 pieces of goose breast in the skillet and sear quickly on both sides.

- After turning add 2 tablespoons butter. Keep turning the steaks and add 2 more tablespoons butter. Cook for 5 minutes only. They should be pink inside. Season with salt and pepper. Remove steaks to warm plates and pour the pan juices over the top.

"What is sauce for the goose may be sauce for the gander, but it is not necessarily sauce for the chicken, the duck, the turkey or the Guinea hen."

Alice B. Toklas

Turkey Panne (Breaded Turkey)

Serves 6

1 whole turkey breast, boned and skinned

2 eggs

½ cup ground almonds

2 cups dry breadcrumbs

2 teaspoons grated lemon peel

2 teaspoons freshly ground black pepper

2 cloves garlic, cut in half

Olive oil

Savory Garlic Sauce:
¾ cup olive oil

4 cloves garlic, chopped

3 tablespoons flour

1 cup chicken stock

2 tablespoons chopped parsley

½ teaspoon fresh basil (¼ teaspoon dried)

½ teaspoon fresh oregano (¼ teaspoon dried)

¼ cup butter

Salt, to taste

Liquid red pepper seasoning, to taste

- Slice each turkey breast into horizontal thirds, to make scallopine. Place between layers of foil or waxed paper and pound with a veal pounder or heavy mallet to flatten. Cut into long narrow strips approximately 1¼-inches wide.

- Beat eggs in a shallow bowl.

- Combine almonds, crumbs, lemon peel and pepper in another shallow bowl.

- Dip each turkey strip into the egg mixture first, then in the crumb mixture. Chill for 15 to 20 minutes before frying.

- In a large skillet, pour enough olive oil to cover the bottom. Heat the cloves of garlic and when they are browned, remove and discard. Fry the turkey strips a few at a time until light brown. Serve immediately.

Note: A simple sauce of equal parts of olive oil, lemon juice and a bit of chopped parsley may be served with the turkey strips. Or the Savory Sauce below.

This recipe also can be done with chicken strips.

• • •

- In a medium saucepan, heat ½ cup olive oil. Add the garlic and sauté until translucent but not browned. Add flour and whisk until smooth; cook the roux for 4 to 5 minutes over low heat. Add remaining oil, stock, parsley, herbs and butter. Stir and bring to a boil. Reduce to a simmer and cook for 5 minutes. Season to taste with salt and red pepper seasoning.

Note: Serve hot as a dip for toasted bread points, pasta, deep-fried vegetable sticks, or turkey or chicken strips.

153

Grilled Turkey Burger with Barbecue Sauce

Serves 4

1 pound lean ground turkey

½ cup barbecue sauce (recipe below)

4 tomato slices

4 onion slices

4 small buns, split into halves

4 lettuce leaves

Barbecue Sauce:

1 medium onion (8 ounces), finely chopped

2 tablespoons water

½ cup tomato sauce

½ teaspoon grated lemon rind

2 tablespoons freshly squeezed lemon juice

1½ tablespoons Worcestershire sauce

1 tablespoon cider vinegar

¾ teaspoon dry mustard

⅛ teaspoon salt

¼ cup plus 2 tablespoons unsweetened frozen
  apple concentrate, undiluted

¼ teaspoon Liquid Smoke

- Form the ground turkey into 4-ounce patties. Paint or dab them with half of the sauce and then grill over hot charcoal (mesquite if available). Turn the patties when brown on one side, and dab or paint them with the remaining sauce. Place the tops of the buns on the patties and lightly toast the bottoms on the grill.

- When the patties are done and the buns toasted, remove from the grill and garnish each with a tomato and onion slice and a lettuce leaf.

• • •

- Combine onions and water in saucepan and cook until onions are soft and translucent. Add all other ingredients except Liquid Smoke. Mix well and bring to a boil. Reduce heat to medium and cook, uncovered, until thick, about 30 minutes.

- Remove from heat, add Liquid Smoke and mix well. Pour into a blender and blend until smooth. Refrigerate in a tightly covered container.

Festive Turkey Salad with Cranberries

Serves 6

1 cup fresh or frozen cranberries

½ **cup water**

1 tablespoon sugar

3 cups cooked diced turkey

1 cup thinly sliced celery

½ **cup thinly sliced scallions with tops**

½ **cup drained and halved water chestnuts**

½ **cup diced Swiss Gruyère cheese**

1 tablespoon sesame seeds, toasted

¼ **cup white wine vinegar**

1 teaspoon Dijon-style mustard

½ **cup peanut oil**

¼ **cup olive oil**

Salt

Freshly ground black pepper

Fresh dill sprigs

Whole fresh or frozen cranberries

- In a small saucepan, combine 1 cup cranberries, the water and sugar and bring to a boil; reduce heat. Simmer 10 minutes. Drain; cool to room temperature.

- Combine cranberries, turkey, celery, scallions, water chestnuts, cheese and sesame seeds in medium bowl.

- Mix vinegar and mustard in small bowl; gradually whisk in oils to make a smooth dressing. Season to taste with salt and pepper. Pour dressing over salad; toss gently. Refrigerate, covered, 2 to 3 hours.

- To serve: Transfer salad to flat serving plate and surround with garland of dill sprigs. Garnish top with whole cranberries.

Foil Baked Turkey Breast

Serves 4 to 6

1 fresh turkey half breast (about 2 pounds)

2 tablespoons butter, softened

2 tablespoons freshly grated Parmesan cheese

2 teaspoons flour

½ teaspoon fresh chopped dill leaves (¼ teaspoon dried)

½ teaspoon fresh chopped basil leaves (¼ teaspoon dried)

⅛ teaspoon freshly ground black pepper

1 teaspoon cornstarch

Additional dill and basil if necessary

- Sprinkle the underside of the turkey breast lightly with salt. Cream together the butter, cheese, flour, herbs, salt and pepper. Spread over the skin of the turkey. Place on a sheet of heavy foil. Bring edges together and fold in a drugstore wrap, seal ends tightly. Place packet on a shallow baking pan.

- Preheat oven to 350°. Roast turkey in the preheated oven for 1½ hours. Open foil carefully, and pour off juices, strain. Keep turkey warm while finishing the sauce.

- Measure juices to ⅔ cup, add white wine if needed. In a small saucepan bring the pan juices and white wine to a boil. Combine 1 teaspoon cornstarch with 2 tablespoons water, or white wine; stir into boiling liquid to thicken the sauce. Add additional dill and basil leaves for color and flavor.

Lemon Grilled Turkey Breast

Serves 4 to 6

1 fresh turkey half breast (about 2 to 3 pounds)

Marinade:
⅓ **cup lemon juice**

4 teaspoons Worcestershire sauce

2 teaspoons minced parsley

1 teaspoon fresh grated ginger

½ **teaspoon salt**

¼ **teaspoon freshly ground black pepper**

- Combine ingredients for marinade in a plastic bag. Add the turkey breast, seal tightly and marinate in refrigerator for several hours or overnight.

- Heat charcoal or mesquite grill, move coals or wood to grill turkey with indirect heat. Remove turkey from marinade and place on grill for 1 to 1½ hours, or until meat thermometer registers 170°.

Chicken Hash Club "21"

Serves 4 to 6

2½ pounds chicken

1 cup wild rice, rinsed

2 tablespoons butter

½ cup dry sherry

Salt and pepper

¼ cup butter, melted

2 tablespoons flour

2 cups milk, scalded

½ cup light cream

Parmesan cheese, freshly grated

Mornay Sauce:

¼ cup butter

2 tablespoons flour

2 cups milk, scalded

3 egg yolks, beaten

2 tablespoons heavy cream

½ cup Parmesan cheese, freshly grated

Salt and freshly ground pepper to taste

- In a large kettle or stock pot, cover the chicken with cold water, bring to a boil. Reduce heat to simmer and poach the chicken for 45 to 60 minutes, until tender. Cool chicken in the broth. Remove meat from the bones and cut into cubes. Set aside.

- Cook wild rice in 4 cups boiling water for 20 minutes, stirring frequently. Drain. Sauté briefly in butter, then add sherry and salt and pepper to taste. Remove from heat; set aside and keep warm.

- In a medium skillet, blend ¼ cup butter and flour; slowly add the milk, cook until smooth and thickened, then simmer for 10 to 15 minutes. Add the light cream and the reserved chicken. Season with salt and pepper to taste.

- In a shallow baking dish, arrange a border of wild rice. Heap the creamed chicken in the center. Pour Mornay sauce (see below) over all. Sprinkle with Parmesan cheese and place dish under the broiler until cheese is melted and browned.

•   •   •

- In a medium saucepan, melt butter, blend in flour and slowly add the warm milk. Cook until smooth and thickened.

- Add a bit of the thickened sauce to the beaten egg yolks, whisk to combine. Whisk the egg mixture into the sauce. Do not allow to boil.

- Add cream, Parmesan cheese, salt and pepper. Cook only to melt the cheese and thicken the sauce.

158

Pink Adobe Avocado Halves
with Chicken in Chili Sauce

Serves 6

The Dressing:

1 cup mayonnaise

1 cup chili sauce

1 teaspoon capers

1 teaspoon chili powder

1 teaspoon chopped pickled jalapeño pepper (or other hot pepper)

¼ teaspoon salt

1 teaspoon fresh minced cilantro

The Salad:

3 cups cooked cubed chicken

6 large romaine lettuce leaves

3 ripe avocados, halved, pitted, and peeled

1 medium tomato, peeled, cut into wedges

3 hard cooked eggs, cut into wedges

12 black olives, pitted

2 tablespoons minced fresh chives

- Mix together the dressing ingredients. Add some dressing to the cubed chicken; use just enough to moisten the chicken.

• • •

- On chilled plates, place a lettuce leaf and one avocado half per plate. Divide the chicken among the avocados. Garnish plates with tomato, eggs, olives, and sprinkle with chives.

- Serve remaining dressing on the side. Serve with hot, buttered flour tortillas.

159

Eastern North Carolina Barbecued Chicken

Serves 4

1 chicken (2½ to 3 pounds), quartered

Salt

1 teaspoon sugar

1 cup cider vinegar

1 teaspoon crushed red pepper flakes

- Preheat oven to 375°.

- In a shallow baking dish, place chicken skin side down, in a single layer. Sprinkle with sugar and crushed red pepper. Pour the vinegar over all.

- In preheated oven, roast for 30 minutes and, when chicken has browned lightly, turn chicken skin side up and continue roasting another 30 minutes, until brown and tender.

Chicken Avocado Cutlets

Serves 8

3 tablespoons butter, softened

4 tablespoons flour

1½ cups milk, scalded

2 cups diced avocado

2 cups cooked shredded chicken

Salt and pepper

Beaten egg

Dry breadcrumbs

- With your fingers knead butter and flour to a paste. In the saucepan with the scalded milk, whisk the paste into the milk and cook until thickened; set aside to cool. Add the avocado and chicken; mix thoroughly but lightly. Season to taste with salt and pepper.

- Shape the chicken mixture into cutlets. Roll in breadcrumbs, then in beaten egg and again in the crumbs. Fry to a golden brown in deep hot oil, 375° to 390°, about 3 to 5 minutes.

Note: Turkey, crabmeat, lobster, salmon, shrimp or tuna may be used instead of chicken.

Rich and Meaty Chicken Pie

Makes 2 10-inch pies

1 large chicken (3 to 4 pounds)

1 carrot, peeled and quartered

2 ribs celery, roughly chopped

2 large onions, peeled and halved

Bouquet Garni: 1 sprig each parsley, dill, thyme
   and 1 bay leaf, tied in a cheese cloth bundle

½ cup butter

2 tablespoons homemade chicken stock

2 tablespoons cornstarch

1 teaspoon flour

½ cup milk

½ cup heavy cream

½ cup vermouth

10 shallots, chopped

8 potatoes, cubed and parboiled

24 mushrooms, sliced and sautéed

1 bunch carrots, coarsely chopped and parboiled

6 small white onions, chopped and parboiled

1 bunch celery, finely chopped

1½ cups minced fennel bulb

Pinch freshly grated nutmeg

Salt and freshly ground black pepper

2 packages frozen peas

¼ cup cognac

Parsley and dill, chopped

Pie crust for 1 pie

- In a stock pot, cover chicken with water. Add carrot, celery, onion and bouquet garni. Bring to a boil and cook until chicken is tender. Remove chicken and cool. Reserve stock.

- In a large saucepan, melt the butter. Combine the 2 tablespoons cornstarch with the 2 tablespoons stock. Add the cornstarch mixture and the flour to the butter. Dilute the mixture with the milk and cream. Add vermouth and 1½ cups more chicken stock. Cook over moderate heat, whisking constantly, until the sauce is the consistency of heavy cream. Remove from heat and set aside.

- Remove the chicken from the bones in large pieces. In a small skillet, melt 2 tablespoons butter and sauté shallots until golden and stir into the sauce. Add the chicken, potatoes, mushrooms, carrots, onions, celery and fennel to the sauce. Season to taste.

- If the chicken mixture is too thick, thin with stock or milk, if mixture is too thin add heavy cream. Add the peas, cognac, parsley and dill.

- Pour the chicken-vegetable mixture into a deep-dish pie plate, or individual serving pieces. Roll pie pastry ⅛-inch thick; cover the chicken mixture, crimping the sides tightly and cutting steam vents in the top of the crust.

- Preheat oven to 400°. Place prepared chicken pies on a baking sheet, to catch drips, and place in preheated oven for 15 minutes; lower heat to 350° and bake for 45 minutes more.

Note: The chicken pie may be frozen after assembly. If frozen, put the pie in a preheated 400° oven and bake for 1¼ hours.

Marinated Szechuan Chicken Salad

Serves 6

The Dressing:

4 large fresh basil leaves

⅛ teaspoon red chili flakes

1 teaspoon Szechuan peppercorns

¼ cup grated fresh ginger root

1 clove garlic, crushed

2 tablespoons honey

¼ cup light soy sauce

¼ cup red wine vinegar

¼ cup toasted sesame oil

½ cup water

The Salad:

6 half chicken breasts, boned and skinned

1 large head romaine lettuce, washed and dried

1 medium head white cabbage, thinly sliced

2 large carrots, peeled and grated (about 1½ cups)

6 scallions, finely chopped

Fresh fruit for garnish

- Combine dressing ingredients in a blender or food processor. Process until smooth. Set aside ¾ cup dressing for serving time.

- Marinate the chicken breasts in the remaining dressing for at least 1 hour.

- Preheat oven to 400°.

- On a grill, quickly sear chicken breasts for 2 minutes on each side. Then place in a large baking pan and place in preheated oven for about 12 minutes. Cool and slice into thin strips.

- On 6 chilled plates, arrange lettuce leaves, cabbage, carrots and scallions. Place about 4 or 5 chicken strips over the lettuce. Spoon 2 tablespoons of the dressing on each salad. Garnish with fresh fruit.

Ginger Chicken

Serves 6

½ **cup light soy sauce**

¼ **cup dry white wine**

1 tablespoon chopped fresh ginger

½ **teaspoon freshly grated lemon rind**

3 tablespoons freshly squeezed lemon juice

¼ **teaspoon freshly ground black pepper**

3 whole chicken breasts, split and boned (or 6 legs and thighs attached)

- Combine soy sauce, wine, ginger, lemon rind and juice and pepper in a plastic bag. Add the chicken pieces and seal the bag. Refrigerate for at least 4 hours or overnight.

- Preheat oven to 400°.

- Drain chicken and discard marinade. In a greased ovenproof baking dish, arrange chicken, skin side down, in a single layer. Bake in the preheated oven for 15 minutes. Turn chicken and bake for 10 minutes longer for breasts (20 to 25 minutes longer for dark meat).

Chicken with Basil

Serves 4

2 whole chicken breasts, boned and skinned

3 tablespoons butter

⅓ **cup chopped fresh basil**

Salt to taste

- Reserve the bones from boning the chicken breasts. Crack the bones into small pieces and place them in a saucepan, cover with water and simmer 45 minutes. Skim off foam. Strain the stock, return to the pan and simmer uncovered while preparing chicken.

- In a medium skillet, melt 3 tablespoons butter. Sprinkle the chicken fillets with salt. Add to the hot butter. Sauté for 3 minutes on each side, until just done. Remove chicken to a warm plate and keep warm.

- Add 1 cup of the fresh chicken broth to the pan and boil over high heat for several minutes. Stir to deglaze the pan and cook until mixture reduces slightly. Add the basil. Pour over chicken breasts and serve at once.

163

Chicken Breasts in Phyllo

Serves 8

¼ **cup unsalted butter**

**8 half chicken breasts, boned and skinned, cut
into 1-inch strips**

Salt and freshly ground pepper

⅓ **cup Dijon-style mustard**

2 cups heavy cream

12 phyllo sheets, cut in half

¾ **cup butter, melted**

¼ **cup fresh breadcrumbs**

1 egg

1 teaspoon water

- In a large skillet, melt butter. Season chicken with salt and pepper, then sauté in the butter for about 5 minutes. Transfer to a platter.

- Add mustard to the skillet, scraping up the browned bits. Whisk in the cream and blend. Simmer until thickened. Remove from heat and stir in the chicken.

- Preheat oven to 450°.

- On a damp towel, place one-half sheet of phyllo, brush with melted butter and sprinkle lightly with breadcrumbs. Repeat with two more phyllo sheets. (That is three half sheets per serving.) Spoon one serving of chicken and sauce onto the lower third of phyllo, and roll up jelly roll fashion, folding in the sides. Place seam side down and place on a jelly roll pan. Continue with the remaining phyllo sheets and chicken mixture.

- Beat together the egg and 1 teaspoon water. Using a pastry brush, glaze the dough. Bake in preheated oven for 12 to 15 minutes. Serve immediately.

Garden Stir-Fry Chicken and Jicama with Ginger

Serves 4 to 6

2 teaspoons cornstarch

1 teaspoon brown sugar

2 tablespoons Scotch or bourbon

3 tablespoons soy sauce

2 teaspoons sesame oil

2 whole boneless, skinless chicken breasts (1¼ pounds), cut into 2" x ¼" strips

2 tablespoons vegetable oil

3 large scallions, thinly sliced, white parts and green parts reserved separately

2 tablespoons finely julienned ginger

¾ pound jicama, peeled and cut into 1½" x 1¼" strips

3 medium carrots, peeled and sliced thinly diagonally

4 ounces snow peas, trimmed and cut in half diagonally

- Combine the first five ingredients and combine them with the chicken. Marinate 1 hour.

- Heat 1 tablespoon oil in a wok or large skillet over high heat. Add the chicken and marinade. Stir-fry until chicken turns white, about 3 minutes. Transfer chicken to a platter, cover, and keep warm.

- Heat remaining 1 tablespoon of oil in the wok. Add white parts of scallions and ginger and stir-fry for 15 seconds. Add jicama and carrots, stir-fry for 1 minute. Add ¼ cup water, cover, and cook vegetables over high heat until almost tender, about 2 minutes. Add snow peas, stir-fry until bright green, about 1 minute. Add chicken and green parts of scallions, stir-fry to blend flavors, about 30 seconds. Serve immediately.

Poached Chicken Breasts with Vegetable Mousse and Orange Grain Mustard Dressing

Serves 6

8 half chicken breasts, boned and skinned

The Mousse:
1 egg white

⅓ **cup low-fat milk**

½ **teaspoon salt**

⅛ **teaspoon cayenne**

1½ **teaspoons fresh thyme**

1½ **teaspoons fresh oregano**

1½ **teaspoons grated orange zest**

1½ **teaspoons chopped fresh rosemary**

2 tablespoons minced fresh chives

¾ **cup finely diced carrots**

½ **cup finely diced red pepper**

½ **cup finely diced yellow squash**

3 cups homemade chicken stock

• Remove tenderloins from chicken breasts. Reserve 2 half breasts and tenderloins for mousse. Trim remaining 6 chicken breasts and set aside in the refrigerator until ready to use.

• • •

• To make the mousse: In a food processor, purée the tenderloins and 2 breasts until smooth. Add egg white and herbs and process until thoroughly mixed. Add milk and process until smooth. Transfer mixture to a mixing bowl and fold in diced vegetables.

• On work surface, place the 6 chicken breasts, smooth side down. Pat with paper towel to remove any excess moisture. Divide vegetable mousse among the chicken; spread and roll up.

• In a large skillet, place the chicken, seam side down. Pour chicken stock over breasts, cover and poach over medium heat for 10 to 12 minutes, or until firm to the touch.

• Remove breasts from the pan with a slotted spoon. Allow to cool slightly. Cut rolls into ½-inch medallions. Place lettuce leaves on individual plates, arrange chicken medallions on leaves, and pour 2 tablespoons dressing over the chicken. Garnish with orange slices.

• • •

Continued on next page

The Dressing:

½ cup orange juice

1 shallot, minced

¼ cup chopped parsley

½ teaspoon salt

2 teaspoons whole-grain prepared mustard

1 teaspoon honey

2 tablespoons white wine vinegar

6 tablespoons oil

Lettuce leaves

Orange slices

- For the dressing: Combine all dressing ingredients in a blender or food processor. Mix well to blend.

Parslied Potato-Crusted Chicken Breasts

Serves 4

1 large baking potato, grated

2 eggs

½ cup loose-packed parsley, minced

1 teaspoon salt

¼ teaspoon pepper

4 boneless, skinless chicken breast halves (1½ pounds)

¼ cup flour

2 tablespoons olive oil

- Combine the potato, eggs, parsley, salt and pepper in a bowl.

- Put flour in a second bowl. Dredge the chicken breasts in the flour, then pat some of the potato mixture onto both sides of each breast.

- Heat the olive oil in a large nonstick skillet. Sauté the chicken breasts, turning once, until they are golden brown on both sides and cooked thoroughly, about 10 minutes. Serve immediately.

Chilied Chicken Breasts
with Tortilla Chips and Avocado-Corn Salsa

Serves 4

Chili Marinade:
   2 medium garlic cloves, minced

   ¼ jalapeño chili, seeded and minced

   ⅓ cup freshly squeezed orange juice

   ¼ cup freshly squeezed lime juice

   1 tablespoon chili powder

   ¼ teaspoon cumin

   ¼ teaspoon dried oregano

   ⅛ teaspoon cayenne pepper

   ½ teaspoon salt

   4 boneless chicken breast halves

Avocado-Corn Salsa:
   ¼ cup fresh or frozen corn kernels

   1 medium avocado, peeled, seeded, and cut into medium dice

   1 medium tomato, peeled, seeded, and cut into medium dice

   ¼ jalapeño chili, seeded and minced

   ½ small white onion, minced

   2 teaspoons minced cilantro

   2 teaspoons lime juice, freshly squeezed

   ¼ cup vegetable oil

   6 (6-inch) corn tortillas, cut into ½-inch wide strips

   4 leaves Boston/Bibb lettuce, cut into ¼-inch wide strips

- Combine all ingredients for the marinade in a glass bowl. Stir well to combine.

- Place the chicken breasts in a 9" x 13" glass baking dish. Pour marinade over the chicken; turn to coat well. Marinate for at least 30 minutes, or cover and refrigerate overnight.

- In a small saucepan, bring 1 cup water to a boil, add the corn, and simmer until just tender, about 4 minutes. Drain and put in a medium-size glass bowl. Add the remaining salsa ingredients. Cover and refrigerate up to 4 hours.

- In a large skillet, over medium-high heat, heat the ¼ cup oil. Fry the tortilla strips in batches until golden brown, about 3 minutes on each side. Remove and drain on paper towels; set aside. (Or, spread the tortilla strips on an ungreased baking sheet, and toast in a 400° oven, turn after 10 minutes and toast for 5 more minutes or until crisp.)

- Drain chicken breasts, reserve the marinade. In a large skillet, heat 2 tablespoons olive oil, add the chicken and sauté until browned and cooked through, about 10 minutes. Remove chicken, cover and keep warm. Add the marinade to the skillet, simmer until reduced to ⅓ cup, about 1 minute.

- Transfer chicken to warm dinner plates. Spoon the pan juices over the chicken. Sprinkle with tortilla strips and shredded lettuce. Serve the Avocado-Corn Salsa on the side.

Grilled Breast of Chicken, Yamsticks and Grainy Mustard Relish

Serves 4

4 half chicken breasts, boned and skinned

Chicken Marinade:

2 tablespoons minced fresh garlic

2 tablespoons minced shallots

2 tablespoons chopped fresh thyme

2 tablespoons chopped fresh sage

2 tablespoons chopped fresh marjoram

4 tablespoons olive oil

2 tablespoons Dijon-style mustard

Salt and freshly ground black pepper to taste

Grainy Mustard Relish:

1 large carrot, finely diced

1 medium purple onion, finely diced

2 tablespoons whole-grain mustard

½ tablespoon mayonnaise

2 tablespoons dry white wine

1 tablespoon fresh thyme

½ tablespoon fresh marjoram

½ tablespoon honey

Salt and freshly ground black pepper to taste

Yam Matchsticks:

2 large yams, cut into julienne

- For the Marinade, combine marinade ingredients. Rub onto the chicken breasts, marinate covered overnight.

• • •

- For the Grainy Mustard Relish, combine all ingredients. Let set in refrigerator covered overnight.

• • •

- For the Yam Matchsticks, Deep Fried: Heat oil in a deep-fat fryer. Plunge matchsticks into hot oil a few at a time. Drain on absorbent paper.

- Optional Method: Blanch yam matchsticks for 30 seconds in boiling water; sauté with butter and herbs.

• • •

- To Serve: Grill chicken, over charcoal or mesquite, for 8 minutes on each side. Place Yam Matchsticks on plate. Place chicken on yams with Grainy Mustard Relish on the side. Garnish with a sprig of fresh rosemary.

Note: This recipe was developed by Chef John Makin for Duckworth Restaurant, St. Helena, California.

Spicy Chicken Spaghetti

Serves 8

2 pounds chicken breasts, bone in, skinned

1 cup butter

3 or 4 cloves garlic, minced

¼ cup Worcestershire sauce

½ teaspoon salt

1 teaspoon freshly ground black pepper

4 tablespoons chili powder

4 tablespoons cumin seeds

1 medium onion, chopped

1 pound mushrooms, sliced

¼ cup sliced black olives

¾ pound spaghetti

The reserved chicken broth

Garnish:

6 scallions, chopped, including green tops

1 cup freshly grated Parmesan cheese

- Boil chicken until tender, reserving broth. Cool, remove and discard bones. Shred chicken and set aside.

- In a large skillet, melt the butter and add garlic to sauté. Add Worcestershire sauce, salt, pepper, chili powder and cumin, cook for 3 minutes. Add onion and mushrooms, sauté for 3 minutes. Add shredded chicken.

- Cook spaghetti in reserved chicken broth just until done. Do not overcook. Drain, rinse, and drain again.

- Preheat oven to 350°. Put spaghetti in a 9" x 12" ovenproof dish. Using two knives, cut spaghetti. Toss chicken mixture with olives and pour over spaghetti. Bake 20 minutes.

• • •

- Top each serving with chopped scallion and Parmesan cheese.

Note: This dish keeps well and can be made a day in advance. Good with green salad and garlic bread.

171

Breasts of Chicken with Rosemary

Serves 8 to 10

10 large chicken breasts, boned and skinned

20 slices prosciutto, thinly sliced (the number of slices depends on the size of the slice)

20 slices Provolone cheese, thinly sliced

¾ cup unsalted butter, softened

½ to ¾ cup chopped Italian parsley (flat leafed)

2 tablespoons chopped fresh rosemary

2 teaspoons salt

1 cup dry white wine

¼ cup minced shallots

- On cutting board, cut chicken breasts in half horizontally, into a scaloppine shape. Flatten with veal pounder or heavy mallet.

- Cream together softened butter, parsley, rosemary and salt. Spread this mixture over each slice of chicken breast.

- Place 1 piece of prosciutto and 1 piece Provolone cheese on each breast. Roll and skewer with a toothpick. Place in a roasting pan.

- Preheat oven to 375°. Roast the chicken in the preheated oven for about 30 minutes or until done.

- When done, remove chicken breasts to a warm platter and keep warm. Pour fat from the roasting pan and put on a hot burner. Add white wine and shallots to the pan, scrape the bottom of the pan to deglaze; boil rapidly to thicken the juices. Strain and pour over the chicken.

Breast of Chicken on Tongue with Tarragon Sauce

Serves 8

10 chicken breasts, boned

¼ cup butter, clarified

½ cup dry white wine

1 cup homemade chicken stock

2 tablespoons chopped fresh tarragon

4 teaspoons cornstarch

2 tablespoons cold water

10 slices cooked tongue (¼-inch slices)

Truffle peelings (1⅞-ounce can) (optional)

Salt and freshly ground black pepper to taste

- In a large skillet, heat the butter and sauté the chicken breasts until golden on both sides.

- To the skillet, add white wine, chicken stock and tarragon. Cover and simmer over low heat until tender, about 30 minutes. Remove chicken from pan and keep warm.

- Heat the pan juices to a simmer. Combine the cornstarch with the cold water; stir into the pan juices and stir until thickened and bubbling hot. Stir in the truffles.

- Heat the slices of tongue in the sauce and place on warm plates. Place 1 chicken breast on each slice. Adjust seasoning in the sauce with salt and pepper, and spoon over the chicken and tongue.

Note: Smoked tongue is especially good in this recipe. Don't tell your guests they are eating tongue until they've done it.

"God sends meat, the Devil sends cooks."

Maurice Moore-Betty

Meats

Kenmore seen through the east gate. The mansion and its grounds
today occupy a city block in the heart of Fredericksburg.

Martha Washington's Stoved Steak and Potatoes

Serves 6

1 tablespoon oil

3 tablespoons butter

6 rib eye steaks

2 large onions sliced

3 pounds potatoes, sliced

Salt and freshly ground black pepper

1 teaspoon crushed bay leaf

1 clove garlic, chopped

¼ cup chopped parsley

2 cups chicken or veal stock

- In a large skillet, heat oil and half the butter. Brown the steaks on both sides. Remove steaks and pour off all except 2 tablespoons fat.

- Sauté onions in the skillet until tender, but not brown. Combine onions with potatoes, salt and pepper to taste, bay leaf, garlic and 2 tablespoons chopped parsley.

- Grease a shallow baking dish large enough to hold the steaks on one layer. Spread half the potato mixture over the bottom of dish. Arrange steaks over top of potatoes. Cover with remaining potato mixture. Pour in enough stock to come just to top of mixture.

- Dot potatoes with remaining 1½ tablespoons butter. Bake at 350° until potatoes are tender when tested with a skewer, about 1 to 1½ hours. Top layer of potatoes should be lightly browned and most of the liquid should have been absorbed.

- To serve in baking dish, sprinkle with remaining 2 tablespoons chopped parsley.

Notes: (1.) If necessary, brown potatoes briefly under broiler. (2.) Recipe may be cooked up to 3 days ahead and refrigerated, or frozen. (3.) To finish, cover dish with foil and reheat at 350° until very hot, 20 to 30 minutes. (4.) Any fairly tender steak may be used in this recipe.

Special Note: This recipe was researched by Anne Willan, president and founder of La Varenne Ecole de Cuisine in Paris. She lives in Washington, D.C. The original recipe called for mutton!

Shepherd's Pie

Serves 4

2 pounds fresh beef, not too fatty, cubed

2 large onions, sliced

1 tablespoon Worcestershire sauce

Salt and freshly ground pepper

3 large tomatoes, sliced

2 large potatoes, cooked and mashed with butter
and milk

- In "good drippings" (that would be lard) or vegetable oil, fry the beef cubes. Add the sliced onions and simmer, covered, for 2 hours. Add water as needed to prevent burning.

- In an ovenproof casserole, place the beef-onion mixture. Add the Worcestershire sauce, salt and pepper. Place a layer of sliced tomatoes on top, then a layer of the potato purée. Brown under the broiler or in a hot oven.

Oven Beef Burgundy

Serves 6 to 8

2 tablespoons light soy sauce

2 tablespoons flour

2 pounds lean chuck roast, cubed

4 carrots, cut in large chunks

2 large onions, sliced

1 cup thinly sliced celery

1 clove garlic, minced

¼ teaspoon freshly ground black pepper

1 teaspoon fresh marjoram (¼ teaspoon dried)

½ teaspoon fresh thyme (¼ teaspoon dried)

1 cup dry red wine

1 cup sliced mushrooms

- In a large covered casserole (Dutch oven), blend soy sauce with flour. Add the cubed chuck roast and toss to coat the meat cubes.

- Add the carrots, onions, celery, garlic, pepper, marjoram, thyme and red wine to the meat. Stir gently to mix. Cover tightly and simmer in a slow oven (325°) for 1 hour.

- Add mushrooms, stir again gently, cover tightly and bake 1½ to 2 hours longer or until the meat and vegetables are tender.

- Serve with fluffy hot rice, noodles or boiled potatoes.

Note: This stew freezes well.

Party Steak Diane

Serves 8 to 10

1 sirloin steak, cut 2 inches thick (about 5 pounds)

1 teaspoon freshly ground black pepper

½ cup butter

2 teaspoons dry mustard

¾ pound fresh mushrooms, sliced

1½ cups chopped scallions

1 tablespoon lemon juice

1 tablespoon Worcestershire sauce

1 teaspoon salt

¼ cup chopped parsley

- Remove steak from refrigerator 1 hour before cooking. Trim off any excess fat, then score the remaining fat edge every inch so that meat will lie flat on grill. Sprinkle pepper over both sides; rub in well.

- In a medium skillet, melt butter, stir in mustard, mushrooms and scallions. Sauté 10 minutes or until scallions are soft. Stir in lemon juice, Worcestershire sauce, salt and parsley; remove from heat.

- When ready to cook meat, rub hot grill with a few fat trimmings to help prevent sticking. Place steak on a charcoal or mesquite grill about 6-inches above the hot coals. Grill 15 minutes; brush lightly with part of butter mixture from sauce; grill 5 minutes longer. Turn steak; grill 20 minutes; brush lightly with sauce. Grill 5 minutes longer for rare or until steak is as done as you like it.

- Reheat remaining sauce; spoon part over steak. Slice steak ¼-inch thick; serve remaining sauce separately.

Skier's Supper

Serves 6 to 8

1 fresh beef brisket (4 to 5 pounds)

1 carrot, sliced

3 onions, sliced

3 ribs celery, sliced

Salt and freshly ground black pepper

- In a Dutch oven (round) or French oven (oval) place the brisket and top with the sliced carrot, onions and celery. Sprinkle liberally with salt and pepper.

- Place brisket in a 200° oven and cover tightly. Allow to braise all day while skiing. It can be cooked overnight with the same delicious results. (It should cook 6 to 7 hours.)

- To serve, slice brisket as thinly as possible. Offer fresh horseradish or a sauce made from the drippings.

Maytag Blue Cheese Stuffed Pork Chops

Serves 6

6 thick pork loin chops, with pockets cut for stuffing

2 tablespoons butter

1 teaspoon finely minced onion

¼ cup finely sliced fresh mushrooms

½ cup crumbled Maytag Blue Cheese (about 3-ounces)

¾ cup finely ground dry breadcrumbs

Dash of salt

- In medium skillet, melt butter and sauté onion and mushrooms, cook for 5 minutes. Remove from heat and stir in blue cheese, breadcrumbs and salt.

- Stuff the pork chop pockets with the blue cheese-breadcrumb mixture. Secure opening with toothpicks. Bake in a 325° oven for 1 hour.

Tenderloin of Pork with Raspberry and Port Wine Sauce

Serves 6

2 tenderloins of pork

2 tablespoons butter

2 tablespoons oil

4 ounces fresh raspberries (or frozen)

2 tablespoons port wine jelly (or red currant jelly)

2 tablespoons heavy cream

- Slice the tenderloin into ½-inch thick medallions. In a medium skillet heat the butter and oil and sauté the pork just until slightly pink, do not overcook. Remove medallions to a heated platter and keep warm.

- To the pan juices, add the raspberries and add the port wine jelly. Stir until all is melted and raspberries are mushy. Strain sauce, pushing the raspberries through the strainer; add the cream to the sauce to thicken. Return to heat to warm through. Pour the sauce over the pork and serve at once.

Gingered Pork Loin

1 teaspoon dry mustard

1 teaspoon dried thyme

1 boneless pork loin roast (about 5 pounds), rolled and tied

2 large garlic cloves

2-inch piece of fresh ginger root, peeled and grated

½ cup plus 2 tablespoons dry sherry

½ cup light soy sauce

½ cup red currant jelly

- With mortar and pestal (or with electric spice grinder) grind mustard and thyme to a powder. Rub this mixture thoroughly onto the pork loin roast, and put it into a plastic bag set in a dish.

- In a food processor, chop garlic and ginger root until finely minced. Add ½ cup sherry and soy sauce and pulse to combine. Pour over the pork roast and seal plastic bag tightly. Refrigerate overnight turning several times.

- Preheat oven to 325°. Remove pork from marinade and discard marinade. Roast 20 minutes to the pound or until a meat thermometer reads 155° to 160°.

- In a small saucepan, combine 2 tablespoons sherry and red currant jelly, heat just until melted. Spoon this glaze over the roast as it cools. Serve roast at room temperature with applesauce which has been seasoned with horseradish.

Kansas City Spaghetti

Serves 4

2 tablespoons olive oil

1 onion, chopped

2 cloves garlic, minced

1 pound pork tenderloin or pork chops, cubed

½ pound fresh mushrooms, sliced

1 6-ounce can tomato paste

1½ cups water

1 bay leaf

1 tablespoon chopped, fresh oregano (1½ teaspoons dried)

2 tablespoons chopped, fresh basil (1 tablespoon dried)

Salt and freshly ground black pepper

1 pound spaghetti

1 cup freshly grated Parmesan cheese

- In a heavy skillet, heat the oil, add the onions and garlic just to brown. Add the cubed pork, mushrooms, tomato paste, water, herbs and salt and pepper.

- Cover the pan and simmer 30 minutes or until pork is tender.

- Cook spaghetti in boiling salted water for 8 to 10 minutes. Drain, toss with olive oil, and put on a platter or plates. Spoon meat sauce over spaghetti. Serve with Parmesan cheese.

Note: This recipe was often served in the Kansas City home of Mr. and Mrs. Thomas Hart Benton, the famous Missouri painter and muralist.

Aunt Jessie's Ham Loaf

Serves 4

½ **pound ground ham**

½ **pound ground fresh pork**

1 **cup milk**

2 **eggs**

1 **cup fresh breadcrumbs**

Sweet and Sour Mustard Sauce:

½ **cup granulated sugar**

1 **tablespoon flour**

4 **teaspoons dry mustard**

2 **cups half-and-half**

2 **egg yolks**

½ **cup cider vinegar**

- Combine ingredients and bake for 1 hour. Serve with Sweet and Sour Mustard Sauce.

• • •

- In a medium saucepan, combine sugar, flour and mustard. Gradually add cream and egg yolks. Stir constantly with a whisk until mixture is thickened.

- When mixture is thick, add vinegar and stir.

Barbecued Lamb

1 leg of lamb (not more than 5 pounds) boned and butterflied

1 tablespoon minced, fresh ginger

1 tablespoon dry mustard

Salt and freshly ground black pepper

Flour

1 medium onion, chopped

2 garlic cloves, minced

½ cup boiling water

1 tablespoon Worcestershire sauce

2 tablespoons tomato catsup

2 tablespoons vinegar

1 tablespoon olive oil

Salt and freshly ground black pepper

Liquid red pepper seasoning

- Preheat oven to 450°.

- Wipe the leg of lamb with a damp cloth. Combine the ginger and dry mustard, salt and pepper, and rub the seasoning into the lamb. Dust with flour and put onto a rack in roasting pan. Sprinkle lamb with onion and garlic, put the boiling water in the bottom of the pan to avoid burning the juices.

- Roast the lamb in the preheated oven for 15 minutes.

- Combine Worcestershire sauce, catsup, vinegar, olive oil, salt, pepper and red pepper seasoning. Brush the lamb with this mixture and roast for another 15 minutes.

- Allow the lamb to rest before carving. Slice on the bias.

Leg of Lamb Stuffed with Apricots

Serves 8 to 10

1 boned and butterflied leg of lamb

2 tablespoons butter

2 tablespoons chopped onion

2 tablespoons roughly chopped English walnuts

½ cup fresh breadcrumbs

¾ cup chopped dried apricots

2 teaspoons chopped fresh parsley

2 teaspoons freshly grated lemon rind

2 tablespoons heavy cream

Salt and freshly ground black pepper to taste

- In a medium skillet, melt the butter and sauté the onion until soft; add the walnuts, breadcrumbs, apricots, parsley, lemon rind and enough cream to bind it all together. Season with salt and pepper to taste.

- Spread the butterflied leg of lamb on a work surface. Spread the apricot stuffing in the center of the meat. Bring the 2 sides together and tie with heavy cotton string.

- Preheat oven to 375°. Place stuffed leg of lamb in a heavy roasting pan, put in the preheated oven and roast 20 minutes to the pound (about 1½ hours) or until internal temperature reads: 140° rare, 145° medium-rare, 165° well done.

Lamb Shanks with Rosemary

Serves 6 to 8

¼ cup olive oil

½ cup dry vermouth

Grated zest of 1 lemon

8 cloves garlic, peeled and crushed

8 sprigs (about 4 tablespoons) fresh rosemary leaves (2 tablespoons dried)

Kosher salt and freshly ground black pepper

8 small lamb shanks

Sprigs of rosemary and parsley to garnish

- Combine oil, vermouth, lemon zest, garlic and seasonings in a bowl. In a non-aluminum container place lamb shanks and pour marinade over them and marinate about 4 hours at room temperature or overnight in the refrigerator.

- In a pottery or earthenware baking dish, arrange lamb shanks with marinade. Cover tightly with foil and braise in a preheated 425° oven for 1½ hours or until tender. Baste with marinade to keep moist, if needed.

- Garnish lamb shanks with rosemary and parsley sprigs. Serve hot.

Barbecued Veal

Serves 6 to 8

Vegetable Marinade:
  1 large onion, chopped

  3 large garlic cloves, chopped

  1 green bell pepper, chopped

  2 bunches scallions, chopped, some top included

  6 sprigs parsley, chopped

  ½ cup peanut oil

  ½ cup tomato sauce

  ½ cup wine vinegar

  ¼ cup Worcestershire sauce

  ¼ cup honey

  1 teaspoon salt

  ¼ teaspoon freshly ground black pepper

  ⅛ teaspoon liquid red pepper seasoning

  2 heaping teaspoons small capers

  1 3½ to 4-pound boned and butterflied shoulder
    or leg of veal

- In a large skillet, heat peanut oil and add all chopped vegetables. Simmer for 5 minutes over medium heat. Add other ingredients, except veal, and simmer for 20 more minutes. Taste for seasoning and allow to cool.

- Place veal in a crockery or glass bowl and pack the cooled marinade over it. Cover and refrigerate for 4 or 5 hours, turning it once or twice.

- An hour before cooking, remove meat from the refrigerator so that it will be at room temperature. Prepare charcoal or mesquite grill for the barbecue. Scrape the vegetables from the veal, put the meat on the grill for 15 minutes per side.

- Meanwhile, in a saucepan, heat the marinade. After 30 minutes grilling time, put the veal into a deep skillet or kettle with tight fitting lid; pour the marinade over the meat. Cover and braise in a 350° oven for 1 to 1½ hours. (Add water if the veal tends to dry out.)

- Ladle some sauce over each serving and serve the remaining sauce on the side.

Note: This is an adaptation on a Country Weekend menu from Lee Bailey.

Ossobuco Alla Milanese
(Braised Veal Shanks, Milan Style)

Serves 6

1 cup yellow onion, finely chopped

⅔ cup finely chopped carrot

⅔ cup finely chopped celery

¼ cup butter

1 teaspoon minced garlic

2 strips lemon peel

½ cup vegetable oil

2 shanks of veal, sawed into 8 pieces about 2-inches long, each securely tied around the middle

¾ cup all-purpose flour, spread on a plate or on waxed paper

1 cup dry white wine

1½ cups homemade meat broth

1½ cups canned Italian tomatoes with their juice, coarsely chopped

½ teaspoon fresh thyme (¼ teaspoon dried thyme)

4 fresh basil leaves (¼ teaspoon dried)

2 bay leaves

2 or 3 sprigs parsley

Freshly ground black pepper

Salt, if necessary

- Preheat the oven to 350°.

- Choose a heavy casserole with a tight-fitting lid that is just large enough to contain the veal pieces later in a single layer. Put in the onion, carrot, celery and butter and cook over medium heat for 8 to 10 minutes, until the vegetables soften and wilt. Add the chopped garlic and lemon peel at the end. Remove from the heat.

- Heat the oil in a skillet over medium-high heat. Turn the trussed pieces of veal in the flour, shaking off any excess. When the oil is quite hot, brown the veal on all sides. Stand the pieces of veal side by side on top of the vegetables in the casserole.

- Tip the skillet and draw off nearly all the fat with a spoon. Add the wine and boil briskly for about 3 minutes, scraping up and loosening any browning residue stuck to the pan. Pour over the pieces of veal in the casserole.

- In the same skillet, bring the broth to a simmer, and pour into the casserole. Add the chopped tomatoes with their juice, the thyme, basil, bay leaves, parsley, pepper and salt. The broth should come up to the top of the veal pieces. If it does not, add more.

- Bring the contents of the casserole to a simmer on top of the stove. Cover tightly and place in the lower third of the preheated oven. Cook for about 2 hours, carefully turning and basting the veal pieces every 20

Continued on next page

188

Continued from previous page

minutes. When done, they should be very tender when pricked with a fork, and their sauce should be dense and creamy. Pour the sauce over the veal and serve piping hot.

Note: When transferring the veal pieces to the serving platter, carefully remove the trussing strings without breaking up the shanks.

Note: There are many variations and adaptations of Ossobuco. This is viewed as a favorite and was first published in Marcella Hazan's **Classic Italian Cookbook** *and has also been taught in her Italian cooking school.*

"Looks can be deceiving—
it's eating that's believing."

James Thurber

$\mathcal{D}$esserts

Visitors to Kenmore enjoy tea and gingerbread served in the "Colonial Kitchen". The recipe for the gingerbread, handed down through generations of Fredericksburg families, is supposed to be Mary Washington's, the same that she served to the Marquis de Lafayette in 1784.

Kenmore Gingerbread

½ cup butter

½ cup brown sugar

1 cup West India Molasses

½ cup warm milk

2 tablespoons ground ginger

1 heaping teaspoon cinnamon

1 heaping teaspoon mace

1 heaping teaspoon nutmeg

2-3 ounces brandy

3 eggs

3 cups flour

1 teaspoon cream of tartar

1 large orange, juice and rind grated

1 teaspoon baking soda

1 cup raisins (optional)

- Preheat oven to 350°.

- Cream the butter and brown sugar. Add molasses and warm milk, ginger, cinnamon, mace and nutmeg. Stir in brandy.

- Beat eggs until very light and thick.

- Sift flour and cream of tartar. Add alternately to the sugar mixture with the eggs. Mix in the juice and the grated orange rind.

- Dissolve the baking soda in ¼ cup warm water; add to ginger bread mixture. Beat until very light. (Raisins are a nice addition.)

- Bake in a loaf, sheet or muffin tins for about 30 minutes.

Mary Ball Washington's Gingerbread, 1784

Mary Washington was George Washington's mother.

Serves 12

½ cup butter, softened

½ cup dark brown sugar, firmly packed

½ cup light molasses

½ cup honey

¼ cup sherry

½ cup warm milk

3 cups sifted all-purpose flour

2 tablespoons ground ginger

1½ teaspoons ground cinnamon

1½ teaspoons ground mace

1½ teaspoons ground nutmeg

1 teaspoon cream of tartar

3 eggs, well beaten

2 tablespoons grated orange rind

¼ cup orange juice

1 cup sultanas or raisins

1 teaspoon baking soda

2 tablespoons warm water

- Preheat oven to 350°. Grease a 9" x 13" x 2" baking pan; line with wax paper; grease the paper.

- Cream the butter with the brown sugar until light. Add molasses, honey, sherry and milk. Beat very well.

- Sift together the flour, ginger, cinnamon, mace, nutmeg and cream of tartar. Add alternately with the beaten eggs to the sugar mixture.

- Add orange rind and juice, raisins and baking soda which has been dissolved in warm water.

- Pour into prepared pan. Bake 45 to 50 minutes or until cake is firm in center. Cut into squares.

Lemon Sauce for Gingerbread

Makes 1 cup

½ **cup sugar**

1 **tablespoon cornstarch**

1 **cup water**

2 **to 3 tablespoons butter**

½ **teaspoon grated lemon rind**

1½ **tablespoons lemon juice**

⅛ **teaspoon salt**

- In the top of a double boiler, combine the sugar cornstarch and water. Cook, stirring constantly, until thickened.

- Remove the sauce from the heat and stir in the butter, lemon rind, lemon juice and salt. Serve warm.

Abraham Lincoln's Molasses Pecan Pie

Serves 6

4 **eggs**

1 **cup light brown sugar, packed firmly**

½ **cup molasses**

½ **teaspoon vanilla**

Dash salt

¼ **cup melted butter**

8 **ounces pecan halves**

1 **10-inch unbaked pie shell**

- Whisk together eggs, brown sugar and molasses until smooth and light, about 5 minutes. Stir in vanilla, salt and melted butter.

- Sprinkle half the pecans in the prepared pie shell. Pour in egg-sugar mixture, then arrange remaining half of pecans in circles over the top. Bake at 350° about 1 hour, until filling is set.

Notes: (1.) To reheat pie, warm in a 250° oven 10 to 15 minutes before serving. (2.) Do not overcook or pie will be dry. Pie is best eaten day of baking, but may be stored up to 2 days in airtight container. (3.) Molasses may be omitted, if desired, and amount of sugar doubled.

Special Note: This recipe was researched by Anne Willan, president and founder of La Varenne Ecole de Cuisine in Paris. She lives in Washington, D. C.

Miss Iva's Chess Pie

Makes 1 9-inch pie

1 9-inch pastry shell, unbaked

1½ (scant) cups of granulated sugar

½ cup butter

3 eggs

1 heaping tablespoon cornmeal

1 tablespoon vinegar

1 teaspoon vanilla extract

- Preheat oven to 350°.

- Cream butter and sugar until fluffy. Add remaining ingredients, and beat well.

- Pour filling into prepared shell and bake for 45 minutes to 1 hour, or until well browned.

French Silk Chocolate Pie

Makes 1 9-inch pie

1 cup unsalted butter

1½ cups granulated sugar

3 squares (3-ounces) unsweetened chocolate, melted and cooled

2 teaspoons vanilla extract

4 eggs

1 9-inch prebaked pie shell

Whipped cream for topping

- In a mixing bowl, cream butter; gradually add the sugar, mixing well. Blend in the chocolate and vanilla.

- Add eggs one at a time, beating exactly 2 minutes after each addition.

- Spoon mixture into the baked pie shell. Chill at least 2 hours.

- Serve, if desired, with whipped cream.

Blueberry Cassis Pie

Makes 1 10-inch pie

Meringue Crust:
  4 egg whites

  ¼ teaspoon salt

  1 teaspoon vanilla

  1 teaspoon baking powder

  1 cup granulated sugar

  ½ coconut

  ½ cup chopped filberts (Hazelnuts)

Filling:
  3 cups blueberries (fresh is best, but frozen will
    do)

  1 cup granulated sugar

  3 tablespoons flour

  ½ teaspoon salt

  1 tablespoon freshly squeezed lemon juice

  2 tablespoons cassis

  4 beaten egg yolks

Topping:
  1 cup heavy cream

  3 tablespoons confectioners' sugar

  1 tablespoon cassis

  Fresh blueberries

- Preheat oven to 275°. Butter and flour a 10-inch pie plate.

- In mixing bowl, combine egg whites, salt, vanilla, and baking powder; beat until foamy. Slowly add the sugar, beating until satiny. Fold in coconut and filberts.

- Place meringue in prepared pie plate, mounding up the sides. Bake for 1 hour. Cool.

• • •

- In the top of a double boiler combine all ingredients for the filling. Over simmering water, whisk constantly until mixture thickens, about 10 minutes. Cool then pour into prepared meringue crust and chill.

• • •

- Whip cream and flavor with confectioners' sugar and cassis. Spoon on top of the pie, leaving 1¾-inches around the edge. Decorate with fresh blueberries.

Jicama Tart

Makes 1 9-inch tart

1 prebaked tart shell

1 medium jicama, peeled, coarsely shredded (about 2 cups)

½ cup dry sherry

½ cup water

¾ cup granulated sugar

6 tablespoons all-purpose flour

¼ teaspoon salt

3 egg yolks

2 cups milk

1 cinnamon stick

1½ teaspoons butter

¼ teaspoon ground cinnamon

2 teaspoons granulated sugar

1 teaspoon butter

- Combine shredded jicama, sherry and water in a saucepan. Bring to a boil, then reduce heat. Cover and boil gently for 45 minutes or until most of the liquid has evaporated. Drain thoroughly; set aside.

- Combine ¾ cup sugar, flour and salt in a medium saucepan. Beat egg yolks and 1 cup milk in a small bowl. Stir into the sugar mixture. Add remaining milk and cinnamon stick. Stir over medium heat until mixture boils, becomes very thick and separates when a spoon is drawn through it. Remove cinnamon stick.

- Add jicama mixture to milk mixture. Cook and stir 1 to 2 minutes longer, until very thick. Stir in 1½ teaspoons butter. Remove from heat and cool slightly.

- Turn mixture into prebaked tart shell. Sprinkle lightly with ground cinnamon and 2 teaspoons sugar. Cut 1 teaspoon butter into small pieces. Place over filling. Broil 3 inches from heat until butter and sugar are melted and bubbly. Watch carefully and do not let crust burn. Cool tart slightly. Serve warm or at room temperature.

Robert E. Lee Jelly Cake

This recipe comes from the collection of Mrs. Crowninshield. The original is written in her hand or that of her mother. The recipe is used courtesy of the Hagley Museum and Library, Wilmington, Delaware.

Jelly Cake (original)

   1 lb. flour

   1 lb. sugar

   1 cup milk

   ½ lb. butter

   6 egg whites and yolks beaten very light and
      separately

Dissolve 1 small teaspoon of soda in the milk. Sift 2 small teaspoonsful of cream of tartar in the flour. Cream the butter and sugar together then add the yolks and then the whites of eggs. Add flour and milk alternately, a little of each at a time till all is mixed. Do not beat much after the flour is in.

Robert Lee Jelly Cake (original)

   2 eggs

   2 cups of powdered sugar

   1½ cups of flour

   Juice and rind of 1 lemon

Icing:

   The whites of 2 eggs beaten to a stiff froth

   1 lb. powdered sugar

   The juice and rind of 1 orange and the juice of 1
      lemon

Bake the cake in jelly cake tins, spread the icing between the cakes and ice with the sauce. This recipe makes two cakes of three layers or three cakes of two layers.

Continued on next page

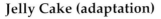

Jelly Cake (adaptation)
A 2-layer 9-inch cake

- 1 cup sweet butter, softened
- 2⅔ cups granulated sugar
- 6 egg yolks
- 1 cup milk
- 1 teaspoon baking soda
- 3¾ cups flour
- 6 egg whites
- ½ teaspoon cream of tartar

Jelly Cake Icing (adaptation)
Makes about 2 cups

- 1½ cups granulated sugar
- 2 egg whites
- 1 tablespoon lemon juice
- ½ teaspoon grated lemon rind
- ¼ cup orange juice
- ½ teaspoon grated orange rind

- Preheat the oven to 350°.

- Butter and flour two 9-inch round cake pans. Line with a circle of parchment paper or waxed paper; butter and flour again.

- Combine butter and sugar and beat well until the mixture is light and fluffy. Add the egg yolks one at a time, incorporating well after each addition.

- Add the baking soda to the milk, stir to dissolve. Add the flour and the milk mixture alternately to the butter mixture, beginning and ending with the flour.

- Beat the egg whites until frothy. Add the cream of tartar and continue to beat until the egg whites form soft peaks, do not overbeat. Fold the beaten egg whites into the cake batter. Pour batter into the prepared pans and bake in the middle of the pre-heated oven for 35 to 40 minutes or until a straw inserted in the center of the cake comes out clean. Remove cakes from the pans and cool on cake racks.

• • •

- Place all ingredients in the top of a double boiler and whisk thoroughly to blend. Continue to beat constantly over rapidly boiling water for 7 minutes. Remove the icing from the heat, and continue beating until the icing is the right consistency to spread.

Poppy Seed Cake

5 eggs, separated

1 cup plus 2 tablespoons unsalted butter

1¼ cups granulated sugar

2 teaspoons almond extract

1 cup flour

1 cup poppy seeds

1 teaspoon baking powder

- Preheat oven to 375°. Grease and flour a tube cake pan.

- Beat together the egg yolks with the sugar, butter and almond extract.

- Mix together the flour, poppy seeds and baking powder. Stir into the egg mixture.

- Beat egg whites until stiff but not dry. Carefully fold egg whites into the batter.

- Pour batter into prepared pan. Bake for 1 hour. Cool in pan for about 20 minutes, then invert onto cooling rack.

Note: A good picnic cake or for afternoon tea.

Polenta Cake (Tuscan Cornmeal Cake)

Serves 6

The pine nuts and candied orange peel:
   ¼ **cup pine nuts**

   1 tablespoon butter

   1 fresh navel orange

   ½ **cup granulated sugar**

   1 cup water

For the cake:
   ⅔ **cup unsalted butter, softened**

   2 cups sifted confectioners' sugar

   1 teaspoon vanilla extract

   1 teaspoon orange flower water

   2 whole eggs

   1 egg yolk

   1½ **cups cake flour**

   ½ **cup yellow cornmeal (fine)**

   ½ **teaspoon baking powder**

   ⅛ **teaspoon salt**

- In small skillet, melt butter and sauté pine nuts until light brown (about 3 to 4 minutes).

- Peel orange and trim white from the skin. Cut into strips ¼-inch wide. Place orange peels in cold water and bring to boil for 3 minutes. Drain and repeat process. Make a syrup of 1 cup water and ½ cup sugar. Add drained peel and simmer for 20 minutes. Allow to cool. Remove peels with slotted spoon, cut into ¼-inch dice; set aside.

•   •   •

- Preheat oven to 325°. Generously grease and flour-dust a 3½ to 4-cup tube pan or a bundt pan.

- With an electric mixer beat butter until creamy. Gradually add the confectioners' sugar, beating until very fluffy. Beat in flavorings, add eggs and yolk, one at a time, beating after every addition.

- Sift flour before measuring and then mix with cornmeal, salt and baking powder. Gradually add flour mixture to creamed mixture, beating after each addition.

- Add toasted pine nuts and orange rind and blend into batter.

- Spread batter in prepared pan and bake in preheated oven for about 1 hour, or until tests done. Cool in pan 3 to 4 minutes and turn out onto cooling rack. Sift 1 tablespoon confectioners' sugar over cake while warm or just before serving.

La Reina Nobile (Lemon Cake)

5 extra-large eggs, separated

1½ cups granulated sugar

½ cup fresh orange juice

1½ tablespoons fresh lemon juice

1 cup flour, sifted 4 times

1 teaspoon baking powder

½ teaspoon salt

Lemon Curd Filling

Confectioners' sugar

12 candied violets

Fresh strawberries, raspberries and blueberries

Fresh mint sprigs

Lemon Curd Filling:

6 egg yolks

1 cup granulated sugar

½ cup fresh lemon juice

½ cup cold unsalted butter

1½ tablespoons minced lemon zest (the yellow part of the lemon rind)

- Preheat oven to 325°. Spray bottom and sides of two 9-inch springform pans with vegetable spray. Set aside.

- Beat egg yolks until thick. Add ¾ cup sugar and beat slightly. Add orange and lemon juices and blend well. Add flour, baking powder and salt; beat until well combined.

- In separate bowl, beat egg whites until foamy and thick. Beat in remaining ¾ cup sugar until fairly stiff peaks form. Do not overbeat. Fold beaten egg whites into yolk mixture with rubber spatula. Combine gently but thoroughly. Divide batter evenly between the two prepared pans (weigh each pan to be precise).

- Bake in preheated oven for 25 to 30 minutes or until golden brown.

- Place pan on wire rack and immediately run a thin paring knife gently around the sides. Carefully remove sides from pans. Let cakes cool 10 minutes.

- Slice each cake in half horizontally, making 4 layers. Place top layers cut sides up to cool completely. Remove bottom of each cake from springform pans and place cut sides up on waxed paper.

- To assemble, place one of the cake bottoms on a flat 12-inch cake plate, cut side up. Spread ⅓ of the lemon curd filling over the cake, but do not spread to the rim of the cake. Place another cake bottom over the first one; spread with another ⅓ of the lemon curd filling. Top with one of the cake tops. Spread with remaining filling. Top with the last cake top, browned side up.

Continued on next page

202

Continued from previous page

- To serve, sift confectioners' sugar over top of cake. Place 12 candied violets evenly around the perimeter. On the apron of the cake plate, arrange the fresh berries and mint sprigs.

• • •

- Strain egg yolks into a heavy saucepan or top of a double boiler and beat slightly with wire whisk. Whisk in sugar until blended. Gradually stir in lemon juice. Cook over low heat, stirring constantly with whisk until mixture coats the back of a spoon or registers 168° on a candy thermometer. Do not boil. Remove from heat and whisk until slightly cooled, about 3 to 5 minutes.

- Cut cold butter into small bits and whisk a few bits at a time into yolk mixture until melted. Stir in the lemon zest. Cool completely.

Note: Lemon Curd Filling can be made ahead and refrigerated. Stored tightly, it will keep for up to a week.

Charlotte Russe

This recipe is used courtesy of the Hagley Museum and Library, Wilmington, Delaware.
The handwritten recipe is from the collection of Louisa Gerhard du Pont, Mrs.
Crowninshield's grandmother. The recipe book was in Mrs. Crowinshield's papers.

The Original Recipe:

"Whip up one quart of cream, and put it in a sieve to drain. Make a custard of six eggs and nearly one quart of milk, sweetened with ¾ pound of loaf sugar, to which add before the milk is boiled one ounce of gelatine, dissolved in a gill of boiling water. When the custard is nearly cold, flavor with a tablespoon of peach water, or any flavor that you may desire. Place a tin vessel in ice and put in alternate spoonsful of the custard and whipt cream. They must be well beaten together and then poured into the moulds in which the cakes must have been previously arranged. Put a few drops of sweet oil on a piece of thin paper and wipe well around moulds before putting in the cake. The cakes can be made to stick to-gether, by dipping the edges in the white of egg. Place them immediately in ice, and keep them 4, 6, or 8 hours as desired."

> *Charlotte Russe is said to have been invented by Carême at his establishment in Paris. It is prepared with Bavarian Cream which is set in a plain mould lined around the sides and bottom with sponge fingers and is served cold.*

Vanilla Bavarian Cream:

2 cups milk

1 6-inch piece of vanilla bean, cut in half lengthwise

4 eggs, separated

¾ cup granulated sugar

2 envelopes unflavored gelatin

¼ cup cold water

2 tablespoons peachtree schnapps or other liqueur

2 cups whipping cream

½ cup superfine sugar

1 teaspoon pure vanilla extract

18 to 24 ladyfingers

- In a heavy saucepan, boil the milk with the vanilla bean. Then remove the vanilla bean.

- In another heavy saucepan, place the egg yolks with the ¾ cup sugar, and beat the mixture until it is fluffy and almost white. Place the saucepan over low heat and, stirring constantly with a whisk, immediately add the boiling milk. Cook, stirring constantly, until the mixture thickens, being careful not to let it lump. Remove the saucepan from the heat before the mixture starts to boil.

- Pour the gelatin over the cold water to soften. Put over low heat just to soften and liquify the gelatin.

- Strain the custard mixture through a fine mesh strainer into a bowl and stir in the gelatin. Set the

Continued on next page

Continued from previous page

bowl into another bowl filled with ice water and cool the custard stirring frequently. Add the peachtree schnapps or other liqueur.

- Beat the egg whites until they form stiff peaks and fold them into the cooled custard.

- Beat the whipping cream to soft peaks, add the ½ cup sugar and the vanilla extract, continue beating until sugar is well incorporated. Fold the whipped cream into the custard.

- Line an 8-cup charlotte mold with the ladyfingers. Pour the Bavarian cream into it and chill the charlotte in the refrigerator for about 6 hours. Unmold at serving time.

Edinburgh Chocolate Flan

Makes 1 9-inch flan

The crust:
  2 tablespoons unsalted butter

  3 ounces Rice Krispies

  4 ounces semi-sweet chocolate

The filling:
  1 cup heavy cream (the thicker the better)

  2 eggs, separated

  4 ounces semi-sweet chocolate

  Chocolate sweets to decorate

- Melt the butter and chocolate together and stir in the Rice Krispies. With your fingers, press firmly into a buttered flan dish and chill.

•   •   •

- Melt the chocolate, cool slightly then beat in the egg yolks, one at a time.

- Whip ¾ cup of the heavy cream and fold into the chocolate mixture. Whisk egg whites to soft peaks and fold into the mixture. Fill flan shell and chill.

- Whip the remaining ¼ cup cream, and use to decorate the flan at serving time. Add the chocolate sweets on top.

Glamis Castle Summer Pudding

Red summer fruits, as are available (raspberries and red currents are preferred)

Sliced white bread (it can be stale bread)

- Line a round-bottom bowl with the bread slices.

- Cook the red fruit, adding sugar if necessary. Then mound the fruit in the prepared bowl. Top with additional bread slices. Set this bowl onto a deep plate to catch the juices. Cover the top layer of bread with a plate to cover the entire top of the bowl. Put a heavy weight on the plate, and refrigerate overnight.

- At serving time, invert pudding bowl onto a serving dish. Serve with any fruit juice which has spilled over the top.

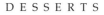
Maine Blueberry Pudding

Serves 6 to 8

2 cups fresh blueberries

½ lemon, squeezed for juice

1 teaspoon cinnamon

¾ cup granulated sugar

3 tablespoons butter

½ cup milk

1 cup flour

1 teaspoon baking powder

1 additional cup of granulated sugar

1 tablespoon cornstarch

1 cup boiling water

- Preheat oven to 375°. Butter an 8" x 8" x 2" baking dish.

- Combine the blueberries, lemon juice, cinnamon and spread in bottom of prepared pan.

- Cream together the butter and ¾ cup sugar. Add the milk and mix well. Spread this batter over the blueberries.

- Combine cornstarch and the additional 1 cup of sugar; sprinkle over the batter. Pour boiling water over all; do not stir.

- Bake in preheated oven for 45 minutes or until a top crust forms which is lightly brown and the blueberry mixture is bubbly.

- Serve warm. Add whipped cream or a scoop of vanilla ice cream.

American Pudding

Serves 10 to 12

3 cups blueberries, fresh or frozen

1 cup brown sugar

6 tablespoons butter

1 cup granulated sugar

⅔ cup butter, softened

Dash of vanilla

2 eggs

1½ cups flour

2 teaspoons baking powder

½ teaspoon salt

2 teaspoons grated orange peel

¾ cup orange juice

Topping:

2 cups heavy cream

6 tablespoons Grand Marnier (or other orange-flavored liqueur)

- Preheat oven to 350°.

- In a medium saucepan, simmer blueberries in brown sugar and 6 tablespoons butter. In a mixing bowl cream granulated sugar with ⅔ cup butter and vanilla. Add the eggs and beat well. Sift together the flour, baking powder and salt into mixture. Add orange peel and juice.

- Put blueberry mixture in bottom of 3-quart baking dish. Pour batter over the berries. Bake for 45 minutes.

•   •   •

- For topping: Whip the cream and add Grand Marnier.

Finnish Rice Pudding

Serves 6

½ **cup granulated sugar**

1 **tablespoon ground cinnamon**

¾ **cup long-grain rice, uncooked**

¾ **cup cup water**

2 **tablespoons butter**

4 **cups milk**

1 **teaspoon salt**

1 **3-inch piece cinnamon stick**

¼ **teaspoon freshly grated nutmeg**

1 **teaspoon freshly grated lemon peel**

1 **teaspoon vanilla extract**

1 **whole almond, shelled and blanched**

¼ **cup butter, melted**

- In a small bowl, combine sugar and 1 tablespoon cinnamon; set aside.

- In a large saucepan, combine rice and water. Bring to a boil over medium-high heat. Stir in 2 tablespoons butter, the milk, salt and cinnamon stick. Stirring occasionally, simmer over low heat, uncovered until thickened, about 35 minutes. Remove cinnamon stick; stir in nutmeg, lemon peel and vanilla.

- To serve: Stir almond into pudding; spoon pudding into individual dessert dishes. (The almond is a sign of good luck for the person whose pudding contains it.) Sprinkle the top of each serving with the cinnamon-sugar mixture. Spoon melted butter over each. Serve hot.

Coffee Macaroon Cream

Serves 6

1½ **envelopes unflavored gelatin**

½ **cup cold water**

2 **cups strong coffee, hot**

½ **cup granulated sugar**

1 **cup macaroon crumbs (or Amaretti cookies, crumbled)**

1½ **cups heavy cream**

½ **teaspoon almond extract (or 1 tablespoon brandy)**

- Dissolve gelatin in cold water. Add it to the hot coffee until thoroughly dissolved. Add sugar and almond extract (or brandy).

- Pour ⅓ of the coffee jelly into a 3 to 4 cup ring mold; refrigerate to set.

- Place the remaining jelly in a mixing bowl set over a bowl of ice water. Just when it begins to congeal, whip the heavy cream and fold with the macaroon crumbs into the jelly.

- Pour onto the coffee jelly in the mold. Chill.

Note: Garnish with chocolate covered coffee beans.

Mousse Au Chocolat Parisienne

Serves 12

1 cup granulated sugar

⅜ cup white corn syrup

¼ cup water

½ cup egg yolks (6 or 7 large eggs)

1 cup egg whites (6 or 7 large eggs)

4 bars German sweet chocolate

½ cup unsalted butter

2 cups heavy cream

- In a small saucepan, mix sugar, water and corn syrup. Bring to a boil and cook until it spins a thread or a candy thermometer registers 138°. There should be ½ cup syrup.

- Beat egg yolks until light in color, slowly add the warm syrup and continue beating.

- In the top of a double boiler, melt the chocolate and butter; add to the egg yolk mixture. Let cool completely.

- To the egg whites, add a scant tablespoon cold water. Beat until stiff peaks form, then beat in the chocolate mixture. At this point put into a stainless steel bowl and refrigerate overnight.

- Whip the heavy cream until stiff. Fold in the chocolate mixture.

211

Sugarbush Mountain Maple Mousse

Serves 8

2 envelopes unflavored gelatin

½ cup cold water

4 egg yolks, well beaten

1 cup pure maple syrup

1 teaspoon natural maple extract (or to taste)

½ cup light brown sugar, firmly packed

4 egg whites

2 cups whipping cream, chilled

1 cup toasted English walnuts, coarsely chopped

- Sprinkle the gelatin on the water; let soften 5 minutes, then set the cup in a pan of hot water. Stir until gelatin dissolves. Add gelatin to the beaten egg yolks.

- In a heavy saucepan, combine the maple syrup with the egg yolk-gelatin mixture. Cook, stirring constantly, over medium-low heat, until mixture thickens and coats a spoon. Do not let the mixture boil.

- Remove the syrup mixture from the heat and stir in the brown sugar, blending well. Transfer to a large bowl and cool to room temperature.

- Beat egg whites until they form stiff peaks. Whip cream only until stiff enough to hold its shape. With a rubber spatula, fold the cream into the maple syrup mixture. Then fold in the egg whites until whites no longer show.

- Spoon the mixture into a 1½-quart mold that has been rinsed in cold water. Cover the top with plastic wrap and chill at least 4 hours or until firm.

- At serving time, sprinkle with chopped walnuts. Don't serve too cold as the gelatin will be too tight and the maple flavor will not be as strong.

Cranberry Fantastic

Serves 12

2 cups fresh cranberries (about ½ pound)

1 large banana, diced

½ cup granulated sugar

2 cups graham cracker crumbs

6 tablespoons butter, melted

½ cup butter, softened

1 cup granulated sugar

2 eggs

½ cup pecans, chopped

1 cup heavy cream

- Wash cranberries and discard any soft fruit. Grind the cranberries. Combine with the diced banana and ½ cup sugar. Set aside.

- Combine 2 cups graham cracker crumbs with melted butter. Press half of the mixture into the bottom of a 9" x 9" x 2" pan.

- Cream the softened butter and 1 cup sugar until light and fluffy. Add 2 eggs and continue to beat. Fold in the chopped pecans. Spread this mixture over the graham cracker crumb crust. Top with cranberry mixture.

- Whip the cream just until soft peaks form, spread on top. Sprinkle with remaining crumbs. Press down slightly. Chill 6 hours or overnight.

"Kissing don't last: cookery do!"

George Meredith (1828-1909)

Strawberries with Mint

Serves 6

3 sprigs fresh mint

1½ pints fresh strawberries

Juice of 1 lemon (about ¼ cup)

- Wash and pluck the leaves from the sprigs of mint. Line the strainer of a steamer with the mint leaves. (A bamboo steamer is especially good for this.)

- Wash and stem the strawberries. Place them on the bed of mint leaves. Steam for 5 minutes over simmering water. Serve with a few drops of lemon juice.

213

Baked Figs

Serves 6

1 pound fresh figs

2 cups brown sugar

1 cup freshly squeezed orange juice

⅓ cup Grand Marnier liqueur

1 cinnamon stick

¼ teaspoon ground cloves

Sour Cream (or crème fraîche)

- Wash and trim figs. Place with "tails down" in an ovenproof baking dish.

- In a medium saucepan combine brown sugar, orange juice, Grand Marnier, cinnamon and cloves. Heat and stir until the sugar is dissolved. Pour this syrup over the figs and bake for 45 minutes to 1 hour at 350°.

- Serve warm with sour cream or crème fraîche.

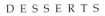

Peach Crisp with Bourbon Sauce

Serves 8

7 large peaches

Juice of 1 lemon

Grated rind of ½ lemon

¼ teaspoon nutmeg

⅓ cup unsalted butter

1 cup sifted flour

¾ cup rolled oats

1 cup brown sugar, tightly packed

½ cup pecans or walnuts, coarsely chopped (optional)

Bourbon Sauce:

½ cup unsalted butter

1 cup superfine sugar

1 egg

½ cup bourbon, more or less, depending on taste

- Preheat oven to 325°. Butter a 9" x 9" x 2" baking dish.

- Dip peaches in boiling water for 30 seconds. Skin and pit them. Slice thin and place in the prepared baking dish. Sprinkle with lemon juice, grated rind and nutmeg.

- Cut butter into 8 to 10 pieces and combine with other ingredients, except the nuts. Mix together with a pastry blender or 2 knives. (This can be done in a food processor as well.) When mixture is crumbly, work in the nuts if you are using them. Pour the topping over the peaches and press down to cover evenly. Bake for 30 minutes or until peaches are tender. Serve at room temperature.

• • •

- Cut butter into small pieces and place in a double boiler over hot but not boiling water. While this is melting, beat the egg lightly and combine it with the superfine sugar. Pour this mixture into the melted butter and cook for several minutes until the sugar granules disappear and egg is cooked. Be careful not to let the water boil. Remove from heat and cool. Then add the bourbon.

Quick Fruit Soufflé

Serves 4

1 cup thinly sliced fresh strawberries

4 tablespoons granulated sugar

1½ tablespoons cognac (or Grand Marnier)

4 eggs, separated

¼ cup additional granulated sugar

- Mix together the strawberries, sugar and cognac. Let macerate for 1 hour.

- Preheat oven to 375°. Butter and sugar-dust four individual soufflé dishes (8-to 10-ounce size). Refrigerate until ready to use.

- Beat egg yolks until thickened. Add the macerated strawberries, blend thoroughly.

- Beat the egg whites until stiff but not dry. Fold the strawberry mixture and the egg whites together. Pour mixture into prepared soufflé dishes. Bake for 10 to 15 minutes in preheated oven. SERVE AT ONCE!

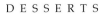

Old Fashioned Dessert Omelette Soufflé

Serves 1

2 egg yolks

1 tablespoon superfine sugar

¼ teaspoon grated lemon rind

2 egg whites

1 tablespoon superfine sugar

¼ teaspoon vanilla extract

Dash of salt

1 to 2 teaspoons butter

Confectioners' sugar

*Optional: jelly, preserves, cooked fruit or fresh berries

- Beat the egg yolks with 1 tablespoon of sugar and lemon rind until smooth.

- Whisk the egg whites until frothy, add 1 tablespoon sugar, vanilla and salt; continue beating until soft but firm peaks form. Fold the yolk mixture and the egg whites together.

- In a nonstick 8-inch fry pan, melt the 1 to 2 teaspoons butter. When the butter sizzles, add the egg mixture. Cover, reduce heat to low, and cook 3 to 5 minutes, or until bottom is crusted. Remove the cover, fold the omelette in half, sprinkle with confectioners' sugar and serve on a warm plate.

*Variations: When you uncover the omelette, spoon jelly, preserves, cooked fruit, or fresh berries on ½ of the omelette, fold over and slide omelette onto the warm plate.

Fresh Mint Sherbet

Serves 8

¾ **cup granulated sugar**

1 **cup water**

1½ **cups fresh mint leaves**

½ **cup fresh lemon juice**

2 **egg whites**

¼ **cup granulated sugar**

- In small saucepan, combine ¾ cup sugar and water; boil until sugar is dissolved.

- Mince mint in food processor; add to hot sugar mixture. Cool covered. Stir in lemon juice. Strain, discard mint leaves.

- Pour mixture into metal pan; freeze until mushy.

- Beat egg whites until foamy. Add ¼ cup sugar, 1 tablespoon at a time, beating until mixture is stiff and glossy.

- Pour mushy mint ice into a chilled bowl; fold in the egg white mixture, blending until smooth.

- Return to metal pan and freeze. At serving time, garnish with fresh mint leaves.

Note: A between course refresher or a summer dessert.

Carolyn's Blueberry Delight

Makes 2 cups

   1½ teaspoons unsalted butter

   1 pint (2 cups) fresh blueberries

   1 tablespoon sugar

- In a heavy medium sized skillet, heat the butter over moderate heat until hot and bubbly. Increase the heat to high and add the blueberries and sugar. Working quickly, shake the pan vigorously, tossing the blueberries with the butter and sugar until completely coated and slightly softened. Serve at once over ice cream or yogurt.

Note: The blueberries may be substituted with 1 pint raspberries.

*"One should eat to live,
not live to eat."*

*Moliere (Jean Baptiste
    Poquelin)*

Cookies
& Candy

Drawing Room.
This is the only room at Kenmore containing wood panelling. A
portrait of Fielding Lewis, Jr. by Charles Willson Peale hangs over the
mantel. Ladies "withdrew" to this room after dinner while the men
lingered over conversation and wine (usually punch or Madeira).

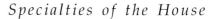
San Francisco Fudge Foggies

Makes 16 foggies

1 pound bittersweet chocolate, finely chopped (semi-sweet may be substituted, if you prefer)

1 cup unsalted butter, cut into tablespoons

⅓ cup strong, freshly brewed coffee

4 large eggs, room temperature

1½ cups granulated sugar

½ cup all-purpose flour

8-ounces (about 2 cups) walnuts, coarsely chopped

- Preheat oven to 375°. Position the oven rack in the center of the oven. Line a 9" x 13" x 2" baking pan with a double thickness of aluminum foil so that the foil extends 2-inches beyond the sides of the pan. Butter the bottom and sides of the foil-lined pan.

- In the top of a double boiler set over hot, not simmering, water, melt the chocolate, butter and coffee, stirring frequently until smooth. Remove the pan from the heat. Cool the mixture, stirring it occasionally, for 10 minutes.

- In a large bowl, beat the eggs until foamy. Gradually add the sugar and continue to beat for 2 minutes, or until mixture is light and fluffy. Gradually beat in the chocolate mixture until just blended. Stir in the flour and walnuts. Do not overbeat the mixture.

- Scrape the batter into the prepared pan and spread evenly. Bake for about 30 minutes in the preheated oven, or until the foggies are just set around the edges. They will remain moist in the center.

- Cool the foggies in the pan on a wire rack for 30 minutes. Cover the pan tightly with aluminum foil and refrigerate overnight or for at least 6 hours. Remove the top foil, and run a sharp knife around the edge of the foggies. Using two ends of the foil as handles, lift the foggies out of the pan. Invert the foggies onto a large tray and peel off foil. Invert them again onto a cutting board and cut into 16 rectangles, or smaller if you prefer.

Fudge Squares

Makes 12 2-inch squares

  2 ounces semi-sweet chocolate

  1 ounce unsweetened chocolate

  ½ cup butter

  2 eggs

  1 cup granulated sugar

  ½ cup flour

  1 cup walnuts, chopped (optional)

  1 teaspoon vanilla extract

  Pinch of salt

Frosting:

  1½ cups confectioners' sugar

  ½ cup butter, softened

  ½ cup cream (heavy cream or half-and-half)

  2 squares unsweetened chocolate

- Preheat oven to 350°. Grease and flour-dust an 8" x 8" x 2" baking pan.

- Melt the chocolate with the butter.

- Beat eggs, add sugar, and continue beating until light. Add the chocolate, then the flour, walnuts, vanilla and salt.

- Pour batter into prepared pan and bake for 15 to 20 minutes. DO NOT OVERBAKE. Let cool.

•   •   •

- In medium saucepan, combine confectioners' sugar, butter and cream. Cook to soft ball stage. Pour over cooled brownies. Chill until firm.

- Melt 2 squares chocolate and spread over top. Refrigerate.

Note: A single recipe of the fudge squares will also fit in a small jelly roll pan (10" x 15"). This makes a thinner bar or square. Baking time will be less.

Texas Pralines

Makes 12 to 15 pralines

1½ **cups pecans, coarsely chopped**

2 **cups granulated sugar**

¾ **cup milk**

½ **teaspoon baking soda**

½ **teaspoon vanilla extract**

1 **tablespoon butter**

Pecan halves

- In a small saucepan, combine sugar, milk, baking soda and cook until the syrup forms a soft ball when tested in a glass of water. Remove from stove and stir in chopped pecans, vanilla and butter. Beat until the mixture begins to hold shape.

- Spread a sheet of waxed paper and sprinkle generously with salt. Drop the praline mixture by teaspoon (or tablespoon, if you want them larger) onto the prepared paper. Top each praline with a pecan half.

Note: Work quickly before sugar starts to crystallize. If syrup becomes grainy, or hardens, return to heat for a few minutes.

Praline Kisses

Makes 4 dozen

2 **egg whites (about** ⅓ **cup)**

Pinch of salt

⅓ **cup granulated sugar**

1⅓ **cups light brown sugar, firmly packed**

⅔ **cup finely chopped pecans**

- Preheat oven to 275°. Cover cookie sheets with aluminum foil.

- Beat egg whites with salt until stiff enough to hold a soft peak. Add granulated sugar, then brown sugar, 1 tablespoon at a time, beating constantly. Fold in pecans.

- Drop the batter by teaspoonfuls ¾-inch apart on prepared cookie sheets; sprinkle with finely chopped pecans. Bake for 35-40 minutes. Leave in oven to cool.

Note: These are meringue-like cookies and are susceptible to humidity.

Damaris' Toffee Candy

1 cup butter (not margarine)

1 cup brown sugar, firmly packed

8-ounce chocolate bar*

1 cup chopped nuts (almonds or pecans)

- Butter a 9-inch square baking pan. Set aside.

- Combine butter and sugar in a saucepan over medium high heat, stirring constantly until it reaches 300° on a candy thermometer or to the hard-crack stage. Pour immediately into the buttered pan.

- Lay the chocolate bar over the top and spread with a knife as the chocolate melts.

- Sprinkle the nuts evenly over the top, press in lightly with fingers.

- Chill. When the candy is brittle, unmold by heating the bottom of the pan just enough to soften the caramel. Cut or break into small irregular pieces.

*Use the chocolate of your choice: semi-sweet, milk chocolate or a combination of semi-sweet and bittersweet.

225

Chocolate Toffee Cookies

1 tablespoon butter, melted

Unsalted soda crackers

1 cup butter

1 cup brown sugar

12-ounces chocolate chips (real chocolate)

½ cup almonds, finely chopped

- Preheat oven to 350°.

- Line a jelly roll pan with aluminum foil. Turn up edges and brush liberally with butter. Cover the entire cookie sheet with crackers.

- In medium saucepan, combine butter and brown sugar; bring to a slow boil until thickened, about 5 minutes. Drizzle (or spread) over crackers. Bake in preheated oven for 10 minutes.

- Melt chocolate chips, and while still warm, spread over cracker-toffee mixture. (It is also possible to sprinkle the chocolate chips directly onto the cracker-toffee mixture, return to oven for 2 minutes to melt chips; then spread chocolate over top.) Before chocolate sets, sprinkle chopped almonds over the top.

- Refrigerate until firm and break into odd-size pieces. Refrigerate cookies in an airtight container until serving time.

Biscochitos (Mexican Sugar Cookies)

Makes about 10 dozen

1½ cups shortening

1 cup sugar

2 eggs

1 teaspoon vanilla extract

2 teaspoons anise seed

5 cups flour

3 teaspoons baking powder

¾ cup water or dry sherry

1 teaspoon salt

½ cup granulated sugar mixed with 1 teaspoon
ground cinnamon

- Preheat oven to 350°.

- Cream shortening and sugar until light and fluffy. Add eggs, vanilla and anise seed; beat for a few minutes.

- Sift flour, baking powder and salt together; add to the creamed mixture. Add liquid and combine until well mixed. Refrigerate for 30 minutes.

- On a floured surface, roll out cookie dough and cut into "fancy shapes". Sprinkle with cinnamon-sugar mixture.

- Bake in preheated oven for about 10 minutes or until golden brown.

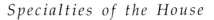
Bernard's Nut Lace Wafers

Makes 52 wafers

½ cup butter, softened

1 cup light brown sugar

3 tablespoons flour

1 teaspoon baking powder

1 cup pecans, finely chopped

1 egg, beaten

1 teaspoon vanilla extract

- Preheat oven to 350°.

- Cream together the butter and sugar until very light; add egg and vanilla.

- Sift together the flour and baking powder. Mix with the chopped pecans. Add to the sugar mixture and mix thoroughly.

- Grease cookie sheets (or line with foil; or, use Line and Bake Teflon baking sheets). Drop about ¼-teaspoon batter onto cookie sheet about 2-inches apart. These cookies spread!

- Bake in preheated oven for about 5 minutes. Check cookies and continue baking if necessary; do not bake more than 10 minutes. Remove from cookie sheets while still warm onto cooling racks.

Pecan Logs

Makes about 40

¾ cup butter

4 tablespoons confectioners' sugar

2 cups cake flour, sifted

1 tablespoon ice water

1 tablespoon vanilla extract

2 cups pecans, finely chopped

Additional confectioners' sugar

- Preheat oven to 325°.

- Cream together the butter and confectioners' sugar. Add the flour, water and vanilla. Stir. Add nuts and mix well.

- Roll dough into a long log ½-inch in diameter. Cut into 2-inch length logs. Place on cookie sheets.

- Bake in preheated oven for 20 to 30 minutes. As soon as they come out of the oven, roll in a flat plate of confectioners' sugar. Let stand in sugar while the next batch is baking.

Ginger Oat Cookies

2 cups granulated sugar

1 cup butter

1 tablespoon maple syrup

2 cups self-rising flour

2 tablespoons ground ginger

2 cups quick cooking oatmeal

1 tablespoon baking soda

1 tablespoon boiling water

- Preheat oven to 325°. Grease cookie sheets.

- In a saucepan, combine sugar, butter and maple syrup. Heat just to melt, but not to liquify.

- Combine self-rising flour, ginger and oatmeal. Mix together with the butter mixture.

- Dissolve the baking soda in the water, and add to the batter.

- Drop dough onto prepared cookie sheets by ½ tablespoon. Bake in preheated oven for 8 to 10 minutes. Cool on a rack.

Potato Chip Cookies

Makes 4 dozen

1 cup butter, softened (no substitutions)

½ cup sugar

1 teaspoon vanilla extract

1½ cups sifted flour

1 cup crushed potato chips

- Preheat oven to 350°.

- Cream together the butter and sugar; add vanilla, flour and potato chips.

- Drop by ½ teaspoonfuls on ungreased cookie sheets.

- Bake 10 to 12 minutes. (For softer cookies bake only 7 minutes.) Allow to cool on the cookie sheet before transferring to a cooling rack.

229

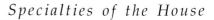

Applesauce Bars

1 cup butter

⅔ cup granulated sugar

⅔ cup brown sugar, firmly packed

½ cup applesauce

2 cups flour

2½ teaspoons baking powder

½ teaspoon cinnamon

⅛ teaspoon nutmeg, freshly grated

2 eggs

2 teaspoons vanilla extract

½ cup raisins (optional)

½ cup pecans (optional)

Frosting:
  ¼ cup butter, softened

  1½ cups confectioners' sugar

  ¼ teaspoon maple flavoring

  Light cream - just enough to make frosting
    spreadable

- Preheat oven to 350°.

- In a medium sized saucepan, heat the butter, granulated sugar, brown sugar and applesauce.

- Sift together the flour, baking powder, cinnamon and nutmeg.

- Mix together the butter mixture and the flour mixture, and add the eggs, vanilla, raisins and nuts. Blend thoroughly and pour into an ungreased jelly roll pan.

- Bake in the preheated oven for 25 to 30 minutes. Do not over bake! While still warm, frost. When cool cut into bars.

•　•　•

- Combine butter, confectioners' sugar and maple flavoring. Add just enough cream (or milk) to make a thin frosting.

Oatmeal Crispies

Makes 5 dozen

1½ cups sifted all-purpose flour

1 teaspoon salt

1 teaspoon soda

3 cups quick cooking walnuts

1 cup chopped walnuts

1 cup butter

1 cup brown sugar

1 cup white sugar

2 well-beaten eggs

1 teaspoon vanilla

- Preheat oven to 350°.

- Sift together flour, salt and soda; add oatmeal and nuts. Cream butter; gradually add sugar and cream thoroughly. Add eggs and vanilla; beat well. Add flour mixture and mix well.

- Shape into log rolls and chill thoroughly. Slice ¼-inch thick. Bake on ungreased sheet, 10 minutes.

Note: As an option ½ cup raisins or dates may be added.

"The cook was a good cook, as cooks go;
and as cooks go she went."

"Saki" (Hector Hugh Munro)

Miscellany

The Chamber.
This splendid bedroom on the main floor of the mansion is hung, in
summer, with dimity, a popular fabric in 18th-century America. The
famous "Four Seasons" ceiling here contains palms for spring, grapes
for summer, acorns for fall and mistletoe for winter.

Fourteen Day Pickles

Yields 12 pints

1½ gallons small cucumbers

1 cup uniodized salt

1 "tin" powdered alum (about 1¼ ounces)

1 "tin" pickling spices* (about 4 tablespoons)

5 cups apple cider vinegar

5 cups granulated sugar

- On the first day wash and slice cucumbers. Place in a large stoneware or enamelware container. Bring 1 gallon of water to a boil. Add the salt and stir to dissolve. Pour the salt water over the cucumbers. Cover the container and weight down the cucumbers with a plate. Let set for 7 days.

- On the eighth day, drain the cucumbers and return to the stoneware container. Bring 1 gallon of water to a boil. Pour over the cucumbers and let set for 24 hours.

- On the ninth day, repeat process from day 8.

- On the tenth day, drain the cucumbers and return to the stoneware container. Bring 1 gallon of water to a boil. Add the alum and stir to dissolve. Pour over cucumbers.

- On the eleventh day, repeat process from day 8.

- On the twelfth day, drain the cucumbers and return to the stoneware container. Combine the vinegar, sugar, pickling spices and 1 gallon of water in a large kettle and bring to a boil. Pour the hot vinegar mixture over the cucumbers.

- On the thirteenth day, drain the cucumbers, pouring the vinegar mixture into a large kettle and bring it to a boil. Return the cucumbers to the stoneware container and cover with the hot vinegar mixture.

- On the fourteenth day, drain the cucumbers, pouring the vinegar mixture into a large kettle. While the

Continued from previous page

vinegar mixture is coming to a boil, pack the cucumbers into clean, hot jars. Ladle the vinegar mixture over the cucumbers in the jars and seal tightly with the lids. (The vinegar mixture should completely cover the cucumbers in each jar.)

*Pickling Spices are generally a combination of caraway seeds, coriander seeds, dill seeds, celery seeds, onion seeds and fennel seeds.

Comment: Katherine Conway Haynes comments that these pickles sound hard to make, "but by doing each step in the morning early before breakfast, it works out quite easily." The pickles will keep indefinitely.

Bread and Butter Pickles

Yields 8 pints

1 gallon medium cucumbers, thinly sliced

8 small onions, sliced

1 green bell pepper, sliced into strips

1 red bell pepper, sliced into strips

½ cup coarse salt (Sea Salt or Kosher Salt)

5 cups granulated sugar

1½ teaspoons tumeric

½ teaspoon ground cloves

2 teaspoons mustard seed

2 teaspoons celery seed

5 cups cider vinegar

- Combine cucumbers, onions, peppers and salt in a large pickling crock, crockery bowl, or other non-corrosive container. Add the salt, toss to blend, and cover with cracked ice and let set for 3 hours, stirring occasionally.

- Drain the cucumber mixture and place in a large enamel or stainless steel pot. Add the sugar, spices and vinegar. Bring to a boil, and boil 3 to 5 minutes.

- Place canning jars and lids in the kitchen sink and cover with hot water. One at a time, remove jars from the hot water and ladle the pickle mixture into the jars. Seal with the lids.

Watermelon Pickles

Watermelon rind

½ cup salt

Syrup:

2 cups white vinegar

8 cups granulated sugar

¼ to ½ teaspoon oil of cloves

¼ to ½ teaspoon oil of cinnamon

- Soak watermelon rind overnight in salted water to cover. The next day, drain and place in fresh, un-salted water for 1 hour. Drain again and boil in fresh water. Remove from water and put in an earthen-ware jar.

- Combine vinegar, sugar and oils of cloves and cinnamon. Bring to a boil. Pour the hot syrup over the watermelon rind and allow to "pickle" for 6 or 7 days (longer if possible).

- Each morning drain the syrup into a saucepan and heat to a boil. Pour over the watermelon rind again. On the eighth day, while mixture is hot, put in pint jars and seal.

Okra Dill Pickles

Yields 6 pints

2½ to 3 pounds fresh okra

6 cloves garlic

6 dried hot red peppers

6 teaspoons dill seed

1 quart cider vinegar

1 cup water

½ cup uniodized salt

- Wash okra and remove stem ends. Tightly pack into wide-mouth canning jars.

- In each jar, place 1 clove garlic, 1 red pepper and 1 teaspoon dill seed.

- In a non-reactive saucepan, bring vinegar, water and salt to a boil. Ladle into the jars and put the jar lids on while the vinegar and the jars are still hot, to form a seal. (If you choose, you can guarantee the seal by placing the jars in a hot water bath and simmering 10 minutes.)

- Let the okra pickles set 6 weeks before using.

Pickled Oysters

1 gallon oysters

1 tablespoon salt

1 tablespoon whole allspice

1 tablespoon whole peppercorns

6 "blades" mace* (½ teaspoon ground mace, or to taste)

1 large lemon, thinly sliced

4 cups white vinegar (either distilled vinegar or white wine vinegar)

- In a large saucepan, stew the oysters until the gills open up. Cool on a platter and drain, reserving the liquid. Cook the oyster liquid and skim the scum from the surface to clarify the liquid.

- When the oysters are cold, put them in clean, hot large canning jar. Layer with the sliced lemon.

- Return the 4 cups clarified oyster liquid to the large saucepan. Add 4 cups vinegar and all the seasonings, bring to a boil. Pour the liquid over the oysters to cover (add more vinegar if needed). Store in the refrigerator. These will keep several months.

*Mace comes dried and ground. It is the outer covering of nutmeg but has a lighter, milder flavor.

Roasting and Peeling Peppers, Chilies

When working with chilies it is advisable to wear plastic or rubber gloves and avoid touching your face or eyes.

- Using tongs or a long-handled fork, hold the pepper over a gas flame or charcoal fire. Peppers may also be placed on a baking sheet lined with aluminum foil and broiled about 1 inch from the heat source. Whatever the method, turn the peppers often, until the skin on all sides is blistered and charred.

- Place the charred peppers in a plastic bag, seal and let stand about 15 minutes. This steams the peppers and makes them easier to peel.

- Remove the peppers from the bag and peel the skin away with your fingers or a paring knife. Holding peppers under running water also aids in removing the charred skin and internal seeds. Pat dry with paper towels, and the peppers are ready to use as directed in recipes.

- Peppers may be marinated in a little olive oil with garlic and fresh oregano.

Green Chili Sauce

2 tablespoons olive oil

1 medium onion, finely minced

6 fresh New Mexico hot green chilies, peeled, seeded, and chopped (or jalapeño chilies)

¼ teaspoon ground oregano (preferably Mexican)

¼ teaspoon ground coriander (or 1 tablespoon fresh cilantro, chopped)

¼ teaspoon salt

Liquid red pepper seasoning to taste

- In a medium skillet, heat the oil, add onion and cook until translucent. Stir in green chilies, oregano, coriander or cilantro, salt and jalapeño or hot pepper sauce. Simmer for 5 minutes or until flavors are blended. Remove from heat.

- Serve Green Chili Sauce over burgers, chops, chicken or almost any other meat, poultry or fish. It is also good as an omelet topping.

Red Pepper Butter Sauce

Serves 4 to 6

4 to 5 medium to large red bell peppers

½ **clove garlic, finely minced**

1 tablespoon finely minced shallot

1 tablespoon olive oil

½ **cup red wine vinegar**

Juice of 1 lemon

1 cup butter, softened

⅛ **teaspoon salt**

Dash of freshly ground white pepper

- Cut bell peppers in half, removing seeds and white pulp. Rinse, drain, and chop coarsely.

- In a medium skillet, heat the olive oil, add the peppers and sauté for 2 minutes. Add the garlic and shallots, sauté for 30 seconds, then add the vinegar and lemon juice. Simmer until peppers are partially cooked. Remove from heat and cool.

- In a blender or food processor, purée the pepper mixture until smooth. Pour the purée into a saucepan and cook over medium heat to reduce to a creamy, thick sauce; stir occasionally to prevent sticking. Remove from heat and whisk in the softened butter. Adjust seasoning if necessary.

Notes: (1.) Sauce may be kept warm over simmering water in a double boiler. Do not boil or it will separate. Or keep it warm in a preheated thermos pitcher. (2.) This sauce is a good accompaniment to broiled chicken, veal or fish. (3.) Fresh serrano or jalapeño chilies may be added for a spicy flavor.

Brandied Peaches

Fresh peaches in brandy sauce are claimed to be an old Williamsburg favorite.
(Then, anything in brandy sauce seemed to be a Williamsburg favorite.)

Serves 6

6 firm, ripe peaches (unpeeled)

1½ cups firmly packed brown sugar

Juice of 1 lemon

1 cup good quality brandy

1 vanilla bean, split lengthwise

4 whole cloves

- Place peaches in a large enamel or stainless steel saucepan, add ¾ cup of the sugar, the juice of 1 lemon and the lemon itself, and cover with cold water. Bring the mixture to a simmer over medium heat, and cook until the peaches are easily pierced with a knife. Do not overcook. Remove the peaches and set aside to cool. When cool enough to handle, peel the peaches, leaving them on the "stone" (pit).

- In a small saucepan, combine the remaining ¾ cup sugar, brandy, vanilla bean and cloves. Bring to a simmer and cook, over medium heat, stirring constantly, until the sauce becomes syrupy.

- Place the peaches in a glass jar, pour the brandy syrup over the peaches, seal and refrigerate for a month. Serve with ice cream and dainty cookies.

Kenmore Fig Conserve

Yields 6 to 8 pints

2 pounds ripe figs

1 cup crushed pineapple (optional)

½ teaspoon salt

2 lemons, sliced paper thin and seeded

2 pounds sugar

1 cup chopped nuts (walnuts or pecans)

Paraffin

- Peel and chop the figs. Combine the figs with the next four ingredients in a nonreactive saucepan. Bring to a boil, reduce heat and simmer until thickened. Stir in the nuts.

- Prepare jars by soaking them in a basin of very hot water. Remove the jars, using tongs, and ladle the fig mixture into the prepared jars.

- While the fig mixture is still hot, melt some paraffin in a small saucepan. Pour the paraffin on top of the fig mixture to ¼-inch thick. Let the paraffin cool and put on the lid.

Apple Chutney

5 cans stewing tomatoes

4 pounds tart apples, peeled and chopped

4 pounds onions, chopped

Juice and grated rind of 1 lemon

2 pounds raisins

4 cups cider vinegar

1 teaspoon cayenne

1 teaspoon freshly grated nutmeg

1 tablespoon ground allspice

¼ cup salt

2 pounds brown sugar

- In a large kettle, combine apples, onions, tomatoes. Add spices, sugar and vinegar; boil 1 hour.

- Let mixture stand overnight. Bottle the next day.

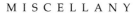
Refreshing Mint Drink

1 cup freshly squeezed orange juice

¼ cup sugar

6 sprigs of fresh mint

1 additional cup orange juice, freshly squeezed

¼ cup freshly squeezed lime juice

Club soda

- Boil 1 cup orange juice with the sugar and mint. Set aside to steep.

- Remove the mint and add the other cup of orange juice and the lime juice.

- Mix 1 part juice with 1 part club soda. Serve over ice in tall glasses. Garnish with fresh mint.

Vidalia Onion Sandwiches

2 large Vidalia onions, sliced then quartered

2 cups water

1½ cups apple cider vinegar

Scant ¼ cup granulated sugar

2 tablespoons mayonnaise

Fresh minced herbs to taste

- Combine water, vinegar and sugar in a sauce. Bring to a boil and cook until sugar is dissolved. When cooled, pour over the onions. Marinate for 2 hours.

- Pour off the liquid and dry the onions well. Mix with the mayonnaise and herbs; spread on thin bread.

Note: For canapes, cut the sandwiches into small squares.

"Let onion atoms lurk within the bowl,
And, scarce-suspected, animate the whole."

The Reverend Sydney Smith
(1771-1845) "Recipe for Salad"

Chicken Stock

5 to 8 pounds chicken bones (backs, necks, wings)

8 whole peppercorns

1 bay leaf

1 sprig fresh thyme (1 teaspoon dried)

6 whole cloves

6 sprigs fresh parsley

1 medium onion, quartered (no need to peel it)

1 medium carrot, coarsely chopped

3 ribs celery, coarsely chopped

- In a large stock pot, cover chicken bones with cold water. Bring to a boil and skim foam from the top.

- Add vegetables and herbs, reduce heat and simmer 2½ to 3 hours.

- Strain and discard bones. Cool, then refrigerate. When the fat has congealed on the top, skim it off and discard. If stock is very light in color, return to a wide-mouthed saucepan and boil to reduce to intensify flavors.

- Cool the stock and refrigerate or freeze.

Basic Brown Stock

5 to 8 pounds veal bones (or beef and veal)

2 large carrots, coarsely chopped

2 large onions, coarsely chopped (unpeeled)

2 leeks

3 ribs of celery

- In a large roasting pan, place the bones and vegetables. Place in a hot oven to brown, stirring occasionally.

- Place browned bones and vegetables in a large stock pot, cover with cold water. Bring to a boil and skim the scum that rises to the surface. Reduce to a simmer, and simmer for 3 to 5 hours. Occasionally skim the additional scum that appears.

- Pour stock through a large strainer to remove bones and vegetables. (The bones can be used 1 more time; repeat step 2.) Cool stock and refrigerate. Skim any fat from the surface.

- To intensify the stock flavor, return to a large pot and boil to reduce.

Note: An alternate method is to pour off all the water after the first boil to remove the scum. Add fresh water and simmer.

Almost Hollandaise

Makes ⅔ cup sauce

1 egg
¼ cup non-fat milk
Dash freshly grated nutmeg
Dash freshly grated white pepper
1 teaspoon freshly squeezed lemon juice
½ cup plain low-fat yogurt

- In the top of a double boiler, place the egg yolk and beat with a wire whisk until turns light in color.

- Still beating constantly, add very slowly the non-fat milk which has been blended with nutmeg, salt and pepper. Place over boiling water and whisk for a moment before adding lemon juice.

- When sauce has thickened, fold in yogurt and heat slightly.

Basic Mayonnaise

Makes about 1½ cups

1 large egg
1 egg yolk
1 teaspoon lemon juice
1 teaspoon Dijon-style mustard
½ teaspoon salt
Freshly ground white pepper
1 to 1½ cups safflower oil

- In a blender or a food processor, combine eggs, lemon juice, mustard, salt and pepper and 2 tablespoons of oil. Blend thoroughly. Then, with blender or processor running, slowly dribble in the oil at first, then increase to a steady, thin stream as the mayonnaise emulsifies and thickens. Adjust seasoning to taste. This will keep refrigerated for about 1 week.

Low-Calorie Mayonnaise

Makes ¾ cup

1 egg yolk

1 teaspoon fresh lemon juice

1 teaspoon Dijon-style mustard

2 small shallots (or 2 thin slices onion), chopped

Pinch of salt and white pepper

2 hardcooked egg yolks

½ cup low-fat yogurt

- In a blender, put the egg yolk, lemon juice, mustard, shallot or onion, salt and pepper. Blend until shallot or onion are puréed. Crumble hardcooked egg yolks into the blender and blend until creamy. If it won't purée completely, add 1 or 2 tablespoons of yogurt. Fold the egg mixture into the yogurt (do not blend, or mayonnaise will be too thin). Refrigerate in a tightly sealed jar. It will keep about 1 week.

Crème Fraîche

Makes about 2 cups

I.

1 cup sour cream

2 cups heavy cream (not ultra-pasturized, if possible)

II.

2 teaspoons buttermilk

2 cups heavy cream (not ultra-pasturized, if possible)

- Combine creams in heavy saucepan; heat very slowly and carefully so that mixture is barely warm, not at all hot. Pour into a jar and cover partially, leave at room temperature overnight or longer, until mixture is thickened. Mix well, cover tightly; refrigerate.

• • •

- Combine buttermilk and heavy cream in a jar. Let sit at room temperature for 1 or 2 days until the mixture thickens. Then refrigerate, tightly covered.

Cooked Wild Rice

Makes about 2 cups

½ cup, plus 2 tablespoons wild rice

1 tablespoon butter

6 tablespoons finely chopped onion

Salt to taste, if desired

Freshly ground pepper to taste

2 cups water or chicken broth

- Rinse and drain the rice.

- In a medium saucepan, melt the butter and add the onion. Cook until the onion is wilted. Add the rice and stir. Add salt and pepper to taste. Add the water or broth and bring to the boil.

- Cover closely and let simmer 30 to 45 minutes or until the rice "blooms" and is tender. Cooking time will vary due to grain size and moisture content.

Pastry Dough

Makes 1 9-inch crust

1¾ cups flour (preferably unbleached all-purpose)

1 teaspoon salt

1¼ sticks chilled unsalted butter

2 tablespoons chilled lard

5 to 8 tablespoons ice water

By Hand:

- In a mixing bowl, combine flour and salt. Using 2 knives or a pastry blender, cut the butter and lard into the flour until it resembles coarse cornmeal. Slowly add the ice water, 1 tablespoon at a time, tossing with a fork or with the tips of your fingers. When dough is just moist enough to hold together, press into a large patty, wrap in waxed paper and refrigerate for about 20 minutes. Roll on a lightly floured surface, turning dough often to prevent it from sticking to the board. Use as desired.

By Food Processor:

- In the bowl of the food processor, fitted with the steel blade, add the flour and salt. Cut the butter and lard into chunks and place in bowl. (Freeze the butter and lard so that it won't soften too much.) Pulse to break up the chunks. Process to cut the butter and lard into the flour, until it resembles coarse cornmeal. With machine running dribble in the ice water, 1 tablespoon at a time. Stop the machine frequently to check the consistency. When the dough holds together when pinched between your fingers, pour it onto a sheet of waxed paper and press into a large patty. Wrap and refrigerate for 20 minutes. Roll on a lightly floured surface, turning dough often to prevent it from sticking to the board. Use as desired.

"…and the wine is bottled poetry."

Robert Louis Stevenson

*I*ndex

View from Dining Room into the Chamber.